British Citizenship Test
Study Guide

The Essential Study Guide for the Life in the UK Test

....

Second Edition

Published by Red Squirrel Publishing

Red Squirrel Publishing
Suite 235, 77 Beak Street,
London, W1F 9DB, United Kingdom

sales@redsquirrelbooks.com

www.redsquirrelbooks.com

First edition published in 2005

Second Edition – Second Impression

ISBN 0-9552159-2-7

ISBN 978-0-9552159-2-6

Edited by Henry Dillon and Alastair Smith

Designed and artworked by
Cox Design Partnership, Witney, Oxon

Printed and bound in the United Kingdom

CONTENTS

INTRODUCTION

Welcome to the second edition of the *British Citizenship Test: Study Guide*.

The study guide is intended for people planning to sit the British Citizenship Test, known as the *Life in the UK Test*. The study guide has been written and designed to help you pass the Life in the UK Test first time.

The study guide gives you all the information you need to pass; everything that you can possibly be asked about in your test is included. The guide also points you toward the information that is most important and most likely to be the subject of the test. Finally, the guide includes features, ideas and study methods to help you learn quickly, efficiently and effectively.

Take some time to read through the next section thoroughly. It tells you about all the features of the guide and will enable you to get as much out of the study guide as possible.

Check our website **www.lifeintheuk.net** for the latest updates to this book and for extra information about the test.

We welcome all feedback from our readers. You can email your thoughts to us at feedback@redsquirrelbooks.com

We hope you find our study guide useful and wish you success in your test.

HOW TO USE THIS STUDY GUIDE

This study guide has many parts and features, however the most important parts are the official study materials. These study materials have been reproduced from a separate publication by the Home Office called *Life in the United Kingdom: A Journey to Citizenship*. The official study materials start on page 21. You must make sure that you read these parts carefully as the questions that you will be asked when you sit your test are all based on these materials. As you read through the study materials make notes of what you think are the key facts.

The other parts of this book support the study materials by making them easier to understand. There are also practice tests that will help you prepare and test your knowledge.

The study materials are divided into seven easy to learn units.

1. A Changing Society

2. Britain Today

3. How Britain is Governed

4. The Formal Institutions

5. Devolved Administration

6. Britain in Europe and the World

7. The Ordinary Citizen

Each unit includes an introduction to tell you what to expect and to warn you about the key themes and ideas to look for in the text.

Revision Questions

Revision questions are provided throughout the units so that you can check your understanding of the materials.

Unit Summaries

A summary of the key facts is provided at the end of each unit. Read over this section to review the main areas you need to understand. Compare these key facts to the notes you have made as you have read the text. Use these facts to remind yourself of the important things you need to know.

Symbols

There are two symbols used throughout this book.

TIP – Read our handy tips and you might save yourself a lot of time and effort. We have gathered a lot of useful information since our last edition based on our research and feedback from readers.

WARNING – Pay close attention to any warnings in this book. Applying for citizenship follows a strict process. We have highlighted many common mistakes that people have made in the past.

Words to Know

The guide also contains an extensive glossary of words that you need to know. These are words or phrases that you will need to understand for your test or are terms that you may need to know to give you background to the core text. Each word or phrase is explained fully, in easy to understand language. As you work your way through the text you can use the Words to Know section to check any terms or expressions that are not familiar.

If English is not your native language, then there are special translated sections for readers whose first language is Hindi, Urdu or Somali.

Practice Questions

Once you've finished revising the study materials, try answering the practice questions. These questions are in ten practice tests. This is exactly the same format as the official test. Make sure you use the tear out marking sheet on page 189 for easy marking.

ABOUT BRITISH CITIZENSHIP

There are several ways of becoming a British citizen, however, the most common is called Naturalisation. This is the process used by a person who wants to become a British citizen but was not born in Britain or has no qualifying British ancestral background.

This section provides you with an overview of the naturalisation requirements. It also discusses the issues and considerations you need to be aware of before you make your application.

Things to check before you start

Before you start applying for citizenship by naturalisation, let's check that you satisfy the requirements. You must meet ALL of the requirements below. This is important. If you don't meet the requirements, and your application is not successful, then you will not get a refund of your application fee.

- Are aged 18 or over when you apply

- Are of good character and sound mind

- Intend to continue living in the United Kingdom

- Have good English (or Welsh or Scottish Gaelic) language skills

- Have lived in the United Kingdom for the qualifying residential period

- Have sufficient knowledge about life in the United Kingdom

Each of these requirements is discussed in more detail in the following sections.

These requirements may change so be sure to check our website **www.lifeintheuk.net/updates** for the latest updates.

Age

You must be at least 18 years old when you apply for citizenship by naturalisation. If you are under this age your application will be declined.

There are different processes for citizenship applications by people under 18. These applications are subject to a number of conditions and are not discussed in this book. You should consult the Home Office or discuss your application with a qualified immigration consultant. A list of qualified immigration consultants is available from **www.oisc.org.uk**

Character

The Home Office will carry out various checks on your background to confirm you are of good character.

Your application must show that you have shown respect for the rights and freedoms of the United Kingdom, observed its laws and fulfilled your duties and obligations as a resident. For example – simple obligations like your income tax and National Insurance obligations will be checked, as will infringements of the law. These checks will include details of all civil proceedings that have resulted in a court order being made against you.

Your application is unlikely to succeed if you have a recurring history of criminal offences or if you are an undischarged bankrupt. The Home Office uses its discretion when reviewing criminal offences. The amount of time since the offence and any reoccurrence are considered when assessing your application.

Future intentions

The Home Office expects that new British Citizens will continue to remain in the United Kingdom. You will be asked to confirm this when you complete your application form. If you do not intend to stay in the United Kingdom after gaining citizenship then you must provide a good explanation. The only acceptable explanation is that you intend to start work for an overseas based organisation that has an association with the United Kingdom. This indicates that you at least intend to continue being an active citizen of the United Kingdom.

Language

British citizens are expected to be able to speak English to a high standard so that they can integrate and participate in British society. If you pass the Life in the UK Test then this shows that you already have good English skills and will not be required to do any further language tests.

Qualifying Residence

You must have lived in the United Kingdom for a certain amount of time before you can apply for citizenship. You must have lived in the United Kingdom for at least five years, or for at least three years if you are applying on the basis that you are married to a British citizen.

You MUST have been physically present in the United Kingdom on the day five years before the date of your application (or three years if you are applying on the basis that you are married to a British citizen). The application date is the date on which it is received by the Home Office. For example if you apply on 1 December 2006 then you must have been in the United Kingdom on 1 December 2001. You should have a dated immigration stamp in your passport from when you first arrived in the UK. This will help you to calculate your application date with confidence.

If you are applying on the basis that you have lived in the United Kingdom for five years you should also have been granted permanent residency (sometimes called Indefinite Leave to Remain) in the United Kingdom more than 12 months prior to the date of your application. In addition, you must not have breached any immigration laws during your residence.

It is very important that you satisfy the qualifying residence requirements. Each year thousands of applications are automatically rejected because they do not meet these requirements. Read this section carefully!

If you have spent a lot of time outside the United Kingdom then this may count against you. The Home Office has clear guidelines on what it considers an acceptable amount of time that you can be absent from the United Kingdom.

You must not have been absent for more than 90 days in the last 12 months. Also you must not have been absent for more than 450 days in the five years prior to the date of your application. If you are applying on the basis that you are married to a British citizen then you must not have been absent for more than 270 days in the last three years prior to the date of your application.

Knowledge about the United Kingdom

You will be required to prove that you have sufficient knowledge about life in the United Kingdom by passing the Life in the UK Test. By passing this test, you will also be proving that you have good English language skills.

Approximately 30% of people fail the Life in the UK Test, so it is important that you are fully prepared. Follow the advice in each unit to get the most out of your study.

 If English is not your first language then read the special language sections in this study guide. Refer to the Words to Know section for further help.

If you still have difficulty reading the English in this book then you should consider attending combined English language (ESOL) and citizenship classes instead of taking the Life in the UK Test. These classes will help you to improve your English and learn more about life in the UK. You can get your English skills assessed at a local further education college.

Other Considerations

Before you apply for British citizenship you should be aware of all the implications of becoming a British citizen. Although you will gain all the rights and privileges of being a citizen you will also be expected to fulfil certain duties and obligations as required by law.

 Some countries will automatically revoke your citizenship when you become a citizen of another country. You should check with your nearest Consulate or High Commission for your home country. Once you give up your existing citizenship you may not be able to get it back again.

Five Steps to British Citizenship

If you've satisfied all the requirements discussed at the beginning of this section then you can begin the process of becoming a citizen by naturalisation. This section outlines the five steps you need to take to obtain citizenship.

STEP 1:
Book your test

Contact your local test centre and book an appointment to sit the Life in the UK Test

STEP 2:
Study official materials

Read the official study materials in this study guide (pages 21–90). Make sure you read our test tips on page 101

STEP 3:
Sit and pass your test

Each test contains 24 multiple choice questions and is 45 minutes long. You must get 18 out of 24 questions correct

STEP 4:
Apply for citizenship

Complete and send off your application to become a British citizen

STEP 5:
Attend Citizenship Ceremony

After making an oath and pledge of allegiance, you will be presented with your naturalisation certificate

DONE:
British citizenship obtained

You are now entitled to all rights of a British citizen – e.g. apply for a British passport and vote in elections

Step 1: Book your test

Your first step towards British citizenship is to book an appointment to sit the Life in the UK Test. Tests are carried out at 90 test centres throughout the UK. You can find the test centre closest to you by visiting **www.lifeintheuk.net/TestCentres** or by calling the Life in the UK Test Helpline on 0800 015 4245.

You should expect to wait a few weeks for your test appointment. This is normal and provides you with a date to focus your study towards.

Step 2: Study official materials

Once you have a test appointment, you can start to study with that date in mind as a goal.

You should now start reading the study materials provided in this guide. Check your understanding of the materials by completing the revision questions as you work through each unit.

 You will only be tested on Chapters 2, 3 and 4 of *Life in the United Kingdom: A Journey to Citizenship*. These chapters are reprinted in full in this study guide.

Once you've reviewed the study materials thoroughly you should check if you are ready to take the test by completing a practice test. You should allow 45 minutes to complete each practice test and aim for a pass mark of at least 75% (18 correct out of 24 questions). The pass mark of 75% is challenging. You should spend as much time as possible reviewing the study materials to make sure you are very familiar with all the information.

 If you do not feel ready to sit the test then you should reschedule your test. Most test centres are happy to do this if you give them reasonable notice. Contact your test centre for more details.

Step 3: Pass your test

Before you leave for the test centre, make sure you bring photographic ID with you. This ID must be valid and not expired. The following types are acceptable forms of photographic ID.

- A passport (from your country of origin)

- A UK photocard driving licence

- One of the following Home Office travel documents: a Convention Travel Document (CTD), a Certificate of Identity Document (CID) or a Stateless Person Document (SPD)

- An Immigration Status Document, endorsed with a UK Residence Permit and bearing a photo of the holder

- A passport-sized photograph of yourself signed by a professional recognised by the UK Passport Agency
  (see **www.ukpa.gov.uk/passport_countersign.asp** for more details)

If you do not bring acceptable photographic ID then the test supervisor will not allow you to sit the test.

When you arrive at the test centre you will need to register your details and pay your test fee. You will take the test using a computer provided at the test centre. You will be allowed to run through a few practice questions so that you are familiar with the test software. Some applicants worry that they do not know the answers for the practice questions. However, this is not important as these questions will not come from the study materials. The whole process leading up to the test itself may take some time due to the official nature of the test.

The computer based test consists of 24 multiple choice questions. Questions are chosen at random from a selection of about 400 questions.

Once the test begins you will have 45 minutes to complete it. This is plenty of time if you have studied the materials. You will be able to review and change the answers to your questions at any stage during the test.

Roughly 70% of people pass the test. If you pass then you will be given a Pass Notification Letter. This is an important document and must be attached to your Citizenship Application.

You will not be able to get a replacement Pass Notification Letter if you lose it. Make sure you keep it in a safe place.

If you don't pass then you will not be able to apply for citizenship at this time. You can take the test again, however you will need to book and pay for another test.

Step 4: Apply for Citizenship

Once you've passed the test and gathered all the necessary documentation you can start the process of applying for citizenship.

Be careful that you correctly submit your application. It is not possible to get a refund for incorrect applications. Thousands of citizenship applications are rejected each year for reasons that could have easily been avoided.

 The most common reason for unsuccessful citizenship applications is that the residency requirements are not satisfied. In particular, make sure you satisfy the requirement that you were in the UK five years (or three years if you are married to a British citizen) before the date of your application. Be careful that you work out your application date correctly.

A good way to check that your submission is complete is to use the Nationality Checking Service (NCS). The service has two benefits:

1. Your application is checked to make sure it has been completed correctly and that all required supporting documentation is attached.

2. Valuable documents (such as passports) are photocopied and returned.

This service is offered by many local councils and is very popular. It should cost about £40 to submit your application using the service.

Check **www.lifeintheuk.net/ncs** to find your closest participating council.

 If you are planning to travel abroad then you should use the Nationality Checking Service to submit your Citizenship Application. They will check and photocopy your passport and return it to you before sending off your application.

Top Five Reasons for Unsuccessful Applications

Residency requirements not satisfied: 40%

- Application sent too early
- Absent from the UK for too long

Age or language requirements not satisfied: 28%

- Applicant is under or over age limit
- Insufficient knowledge of English

Delay in replying to Home Office enquiries: 14%

- Additional information not supplied when requested
- Unable to contact applicant

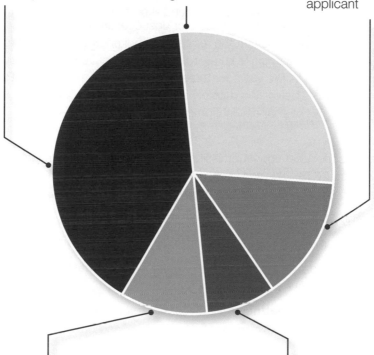

Not of good character: 10%

- Considered a threat to national security
- Recurring criminal history

Application not correctly completed: 8%

- Application fee not paid
- Unacceptable documentation submitted
- Late or improper application

Source: Home Office 2006

Step 5: Attend your Citizenship Ceremony

If your application for citizenship is accepted then you will receive a Citizenship Invitation by post. You will be asked to attend your citizenship ceremony. This is the last step in the process and afterwards you'll officially be a British citizen.

Your Citizenship Invitation letter will contain all the information you need to book your ceremony.

Citizenship ceremonies are hosted by the Superintendent Registrar and usually local dignitaries will also attend. The ceremonies are usually attended by a number of other new citizens. You will be allowed to bring a limited number of guests to the ceremony. After a welcome speech you will be asked to stand and swear the oath of allegiance or, if you prefer, to speak the affirmation of allegiance. You will also be asked to take the Citizenship Pledge. Do not worry – this will be done as a group, so you will not feel self-conscious.

Oath of allegiance

I (name) do solemnly and sincerely affirm …

… that on becoming a British citizen, I will be faithful and bear true allegiance to Her Majesty Queen Elizabeth the Second, her Heirs and Successors, according to law.

Affirmation of allegiance

I (name) swear by Almighty God …

… that on becoming a British citizen, I will be faithful and bear true allegiance to Her Majesty Queen Elizabeth the Second, her Heirs and Successors, according to law.

Citizenship Pledge

I will give my loyalty to the United Kingdom and respect its rights and freedoms. I will uphold its democratic values. I will observe its laws faithfully and fulfil my duties and obligations as a British citizen.

The national anthem will then be played. You won't be expected to sing along, but all British citizens should know the words. It is very short – only 33 words long.

God Save the Queen

God save our gracious Queen,

Long live our noble Queen,

God save the Queen:

Send her victorious,

Happy and glorious,

Long to reign over us:

God save the Queen.

Finally, you will be presented with your citizenship certificate and an information pack. Many people like to remember this formal occasion and take photographs – this is definitely encouraged! It has taken a long time to get to this point so make sure you enjoy it.

 Professional photographers may attend your ceremony and offer good quality photographs. Alternatively if you bring your own camera there will be many people at the event who will be happy to take your photograph.

Now that you are officially a British citizen, you can apply for a British passport. This is a relatively simple matter and only requires one form to be completed. You should only need to attach the following additional pieces of information to your application –

• Two passport photos

Make sure your photographs comply with new biometric regulations. There are strict guidelines for photographs and it is recommend that you visit an experienced passport photo retailer to have your photograph taken.

- The passport you used to arrive in the UK. It does not matter if this has expired

- You will also need to find a counter signatory. This is someone who will confirm your identity and vouch for the declarations you've made

- Your Certificate of Naturalisation

There are several different ways that you can submit your passport application. These have different turnaround times and fees. Full details of these fees will be included with your application form.

Look out for the 'Check and Send' service that is available at selected Post Offices and Worldchoice travel agents throughout the UK. This is very popular – almost half of all people making a UK Passport application use this service. Your application is checked for errors and given priority treatment by the UK Passport Service. The service costs £5 and includes the postage costs for your application.

STUDY MATERIALS

The following sections contain all the official study
material that you need to revise for the test.
If you'd like to learn more about any of the topics
discussed in this section then visit
www.lifeintheuk.net

UNIT 1: A CHANGING SOCIETY

In this unit you will learn about how British society has changed in recent times. The unit mainly focuses on how different groups have contributed to society since the end of the Second World War. When reading the section on migration to Britain, be sure to think about why people wanted to come to the country, but also consider why Britain wanted and needed new immigrants. The section on the role of women in society explains how women have gained more rights and responsibilities. Make sure you concentrate on how women have become more active in politics, education and the workplace. Also think about differences that have developed in how women contribute in their more traditional family roles, especially in terms of childcare. When reading the section on children and young people think about how families have changed in Britain. It is also important to focus on the challenges that face children and young people today as they progress through the education system and become young adults.

There are a lot of key dates to revise in this section. These are summarised along with other key dates in the Timeline of British History on page 91

A CHANGING SOCIETY

Migration to Britain

If we go back far enough in time, almost everyone living in Britain today may be seen to have their origins elsewhere. We are a nation of immigrants – able to trace our roots to countries throughout Europe, Russia, the Middle East, Africa, Asia and the Caribbean. In the past immigrant groups came to invade and to seize land. More recently, people have come to Britain to find safety and in search of jobs and a better life.

Britain is proud of its tradition of providing a safe haven for people fleeing persecution and conflict. In the sixteenth and seventeenth centuries, Protestant Huguenots from France came to Britain to escape religious persecution. The terrible famine in Ireland in the mid 1840s led to a surge of migration to the British mainland, where Irish labourers provided much of the workforce for the construction of canals and railways.

Between 1880–1910, large numbers of Jewish people came to Britain from what are now Poland, Ukraine, and Belarus to escape the violence they faced at home. Unhappily, in the 1930s, fewer were able to leave Germany and central Europe in time to escape the Nazi Holocaust, which claimed the lives of 6 million people.

Migration since 1945

At the end of the Second World War, there was the huge task of rebuilding Britain after six years of war. With not enough people available for work, the British government encouraged workers from other parts of Europe to help with the process of reconstruction. In 1948, the invitation was extended to people in Ireland and the West Indies.

A shortage of labour in Britain continued throughout the 1950s and some UK industries launched advertising campaigns to attract workers from overseas. Centres were set up in the West Indies to recruit bus crews, and textile and engineering firms in the north of England and the Midlands sent agents to find workers in India and Pakistan. For about 25 years people from the West Indies, India, Pakistan and later Bangladesh, travelled to work and settle in Britain.

In the 1970s migration from these areas fell after the Government passed new laws restricting immigration to Britain. However, during this period, Britain admitted 28,000 people of Indian origin who had been forced to leave Uganda, and 22,000 refugees from South East Asia. In the 1980s, the largest immigrant groups were from the United States, Australia, South Africa, New Zealand, Hong Kong, Singapore and Malaysia.

With the fall of the Iron Curtain and the break-up of the Soviet Union in the late 1980s and early 90s, other groups began to come to Britain, seeking a new and safer way of life. Since 1994 there has been a rise in the numbers moving to Britain from Europe, the Middle East, Asia, Africa and the Indian sub-continent, many of whom have sought political asylum. Migrants to Britain, however, face increasingly tighter controls, as the Government attempts to prevent unauthorised immigration and to examine more closely the claims of those seeking asylum.

REVISION QUESTIONS

Check your understanding of this unit by completing the questions below. Check your answers on page 182

1 List some of the reasons why migrants have come to the UK

ANSWER:

2 In 1948, what were immigrants from Ireland and the West Indies invited into the UK to do?

ANSWER:

3 What work did migrant Irish labourers do during the Irish famine in the mid 1840s?

ANSWER:

4 Why did Protestant Huguenots from France come to Britain?

ANSWER:

5 Name three countries that Jewish people migrated to the UK from, to escape persecution during 1880–1910

ANSWER:

6 Why did large numbers of Jewish people come to Britain during 1880 to 1910?

ANSWER:

7 Which countries were invited to provide immigrant workers to help British reconstruction after the Second World War?

ANSWER:

8 During the 1950s, bus driver recruitment centres were set up in which area?

ANSWER:

9 During the 1950s, textile and engineering firms from the UK sent recruitment agents to which two countries?

ANSWER:

10 Name the seven largest immigrant groups to the UK during the 1980s

ANSWER:

11 Name the two places that the UK admitted refugees from during the 1970s
ANSWER: ....

Women in Britain today

Women in Britain make up 51 per cent of the population, and 45 per cent of the workforce. Girls, as a whole, leave school today with better qualifications than boys, and there are now more women than men at university. Employment opportunities for women now are much greater than they were in the past. Although women continue to be employed in traditionally female areas, such as health care, teaching, secretarial, and sales, there is strong evidence that attitudes are changing and that women are doing a much wider range of work than before.

Research shows that today very few people believe that women in Britain should stay at home and not go out to work. Today, almost three-quarters of women with children of school age are in paid work.

In many households, women continue to have a major share in childcare and housework, but here too there is evidence of greater equality, with fathers taking an increasing role in raising the family and household chores. Despite this progress, many argue that more needs to be done to achieve greater equality between women and men – particularly in the workplace. Women in Britain do not have the same access as men to promotion and better-paid jobs, and the average hourly rate of pay for women is about 20 per cent lower than it is for men.

UK population by gender

Male 49% Female 51%

UK Workforce

Male 55% Female 45%

The changing role of women

In nineteenth century Britain, families were usually large and, in most households, men, women, and children all contributed towards the family wage. Although they were economically very important, women in Britain had fewer rights in law than men. Until 1857, a married woman had no right to divorce her husband, and until 1882 a woman's earnings, along with any property or money she brought to the marriage, automatically belonged to her husband.

In the late nineteenth and early twentieth centuries, an increasing number of women campaigned and demonstrated for greater rights and, in particular, the right to vote. However, the protests and demonstrations were halted during the First World War, as women joined in the war effort and took on a much greater variety of work than they had done before. Women (over the age of 30) were finally given the right to vote and to stand for election for Parliament after the War had ended in 1918. It wasn't until 1928 that women in Britain received voting rights at the same age as men.

Despite these improvements, women still faced discrimination in the workplace. When a woman married, it was quite common for her to be asked to leave work by her employer. Many jobs were closed to women, and women found it very difficult to enter university. The 1960s and 70s saw increasing pressure from women for equal rights and, during this period, laws were passed giving women the right to equal pay and prohibiting employers from discriminating against women because of their sex.

Children, family and young people

In Britain there are almost 15 million children and young people up to the age of 19. This represents almost a quarter of the UK population. Young people are considered to be a group with their own identity, interests, and fashions that in some ways distinguish them from older people. Generally speaking, once they reach adulthood, children tend to move away from the family home, but this varies from one family and one community to another. Most children in Britain receive weekly pocket money from their parents, and many get more for doing jobs around the house.

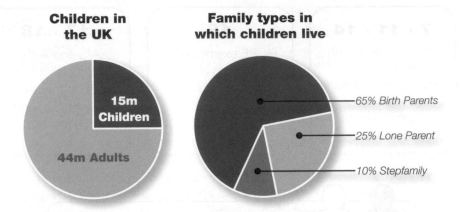

Children in the UK

15m Children

44m Adults

Family types in which children live

65% Birth Parents

25% Lone Parent

10% Stepfamily

Children today in the UK do not play outside the home as much as they did in the past. Home entertainment, such as television, videos and computers, are seen as part of the reason for this, but so also is an increased concern for children's safety. Incidents of child molestation by strangers are often reported in great detail, but there is no evidence that dangers of this kind are increasing.

As a result of changing attitudes towards divorce and separation, family patterns in Britain have also changed considerably in the last 20 years. Today while 65 per cent of children live with both birth parents, almost 25 per cent live in lone parent families, and 10 per cent live within a stepfamily.

Education

The Government places great importance on the need to assess and test pupils in order to know what they have achieved. Compulsory testing takes place at the ages of seven, eleven and fourteen in England and Scotland (but not in Wales where more informal methods of assessment are favoured). These tests help to give parents a good indication of their children's progress and children know the subjects they are doing well and those that need extra attention.

Most young people take GCSE (General Certificate of Secondary Education) examinations at sixteen, and many take vocational qualifications, A/S and A levels (Advanced levels), at seventeen and eighteen.

7 · 11 · 14

Compulsory testing of children in England and Scotland takes place at the ages of seven, eleven and fourteen

16

GCSE examinations are taken at age sixteen

17 · 18

A/S and A level examinations are taken at the ages of seventeen and eighteen

One in three young people undertake higher education after they leave school

16

Tobacco cannot be sold to anyone under the age of 16

18

Alcohol cannot be sold to anyone under the age of 18

18

Young people can vote from the age of 18

One in three young people now move onto higher education after school. The Government aim is to reach one in two. Of those that do, some defer their university entrance by taking a year out. This often includes periods doing voluntary work, travelling overseas, or earning money to pay for fees and living expenses at university.

Work

It is now common for young people to have a part-time job whilst they are still at school. Recent estimates suggest that there are two million children at work at any one time. The most common jobs are newspaper delivery and work in supermarkets and newsagents. Many parents believe that part-time work of this kind helps children to become more independent, as well as providing them (and sometimes their family) with extra income.

It is important to note, however, that the employment of children is strictly controlled by law, and that there are concerns for the safety of children who work illegally or are not properly supervised.

Health hazards

Many parents in Britain worry that their children may misuse addictive substances and drugs in some way.

Cigarette consumption in Britain has fallen significantly and now only a minority of the population smoke. Restrictions are planned against smoking in public places. Smoking has declined amongst young people as well as adults, although statistics show that girls smoke more than boys. Tobacco, by law, should not be sold to anyone under the age of 16.

Alcohol abuse is a problem. Although young people below the age of 18 are not allowed by law to buy alcohol, there is concern in Britain over the age at which some young people start drinking, and the amount of alcohol that they consume in one session or 'binge'. Increasing penalties including on-the-spot fines are being introduced to help control this.

Controlled drugs are illegal drugs. It is an offence in Britain to possess, produce, or supply substances such as heroin, cocaine, ecstasy, amphetamines, and cannabis. However, current statistics indicate that half of young adults, and about a third of the population as a whole, have used illegal drugs at one time or another – if sometimes only as an experiment.

There is a well-established link between the use of hard drugs (eg crack cocaine and heroin) and crime, and it is widely accepted that drug misuse carries a huge social and financial cost to the country. Much crime, such as burglary or stealing in the street by threat or violence (called mugging) is associated with wanting money for drugs. The task of finding an effective way of dealing with this problem is an important issue facing British society.

Young people's attitudes and action

Young people in Britain are able to vote in elections from the age of 18. However, in the 2001 general election, only one in five potential first-time voters actually cast their vote, and there has been a great debate over the reasons for this. Researchers have concluded that one reason is young people's distrust of politicians and the political process.

Although many young people show little interest in party politics, there is strong evidence that they are interested in some specific political issues. Those who commonly say they are not interested in politics at all often express strong concern about environmental issues and cruelty to animals.

A survey of the attitudes of young people in England and Wales in 2003 revealed that crime, drugs, war/terrorism, racism, and health were the five most important issues that they felt Britain faced today. The same survey asked young people about their participation in political and community events. It was reported that 86 per cent of young people had taken part in some form of community activity over the past year. 50 per cent had taken part in fund-raising or collecting money for charity.

REVISION QUESTIONS

Check your understanding of this unit by completing the questions below. Check your answers on page 182

12	What year did women gain the right to divorce their husband in the UK?
	ANSWER:
13	What year did women first get the right to vote?
	ANSWER:
14	In what year did women get the right to vote at the same age as men?
	ANSWER:
15	Are there more men or women in study at university?
	ANSWER:
16	What percentage of the workforce are women?
	ANSWER:
17	What proportion of women with children (of school age) also work?
	ANSWER:
18	What is the percentage difference in pay between male and female hourly pay rates?
	ANSWER:
19	How often do most children in the UK receive their pocket money?
	ANSWER:

20	What percentage of children in the UK live with both birth parents?
	ANSWER:
21	What percentage of children do not live with both birth parents (i.e. live in single parent families or stepfamilies)?
	ANSWER:
22	How many young people (up to the age of 19) are there in the UK?
	ANSWER:
23	At what ages do children take compulsory tests at school?
	ANSWER:
24	What proportion of young people enrol to go on to higher education?
	ANSWER:
25	How many children (under 18) are estimated to be working in the UK at any time?
	ANSWER:
26	What are the minimum ages for buying alcohol and tobacco?
	ANSWER:
27	In the 2001 general election, what proportion of first time voters actually cast their vote?
	ANSWER:

UNIT 1 SUMMARY: A CHANGING SOCIETY

In the Life in the UK Test you could be asked questions about anything included in this unit, but some of the key facts you should remember are:

- In 1948 the British government invited workers from Ireland and the West Indies to reconstruct the country after the Second World War

- In the 1950s continued labour shortages in various industries resulted in active recruitment in the West Indies, India and Pakistan

- In the 1970s new laws were passed restricting immigration. However, during this period, 28,000 refugees were admitted from Uganda and 22,000 from South East Asia

- Since 1994 there has been a rise in people coming to Britain from Europe, the Middle East, Asia, Africa and the Indian sub-continent, many of whom have sought political asylum

- Until 1857 a woman could not divorce her husband

- Until 1882 all property and money in a marriage belonged to the husband

- In 1918 women over the age of 30 received the right to vote and to stand for election to parliament

- In 1928 women received the right to vote from the same age as men

- On the whole, girls leave school with better qualifications than boys

- Women make up 45% of the workforce

- There are more women than men in university

- Almost three quarters of women, with children of school age, are in paid work

- The average hourly wage of women is about 20% lower than men

- There are 15 million children and young people in Britain under the age of 19

- 65% of children live with their birth parents; 25% of children live in a lone parent family; 10% of children live in a stepfamily

- Compulsory testing of children in England and Scotland takes place at the ages of seven, eleven and fourteen

- GCSE examinations are taken at age sixteen; A/S and A level examinations are taken at seventeen and eighteen

- One in three young people undertake higher education after they leave school
- Tobacco cannot be sold to anyone under the age of 16
- Alcohol cannot be sold to anyone under the age of 18
- Young people can vote from the age of 18

UNIT 2
BRITAIN TODAY: A PROFILE

In this unit you will learn about British society as it is today. The unit focuses on the people who live in the country now and the things that make them who they are, such as ethnicity, religions, traditions and customs. You should concentrate on where different groups live, particularly various ethnic groups. Britain is a country with a long history and you should note that religions, traditions and customs have developed in many ways in many places.

You should make sure that you can remember all the festivals and special days that are celebrated in the country. These are summarised in the British Calendar on page 92

BRITAIN TODAY: A PROFILE

Population

In 2001, the population of the United Kingdom was recorded at just under 59 million people.

United Kingdom Population 2001

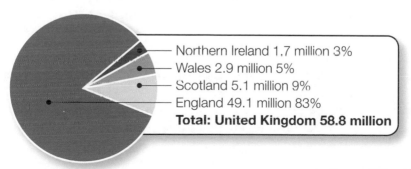

Northern Ireland 1.7 million 3%
Wales 2.9 million 5%
Scotland 5.1 million 9%
England 49.1 million 83%
Total: United Kingdom 58.8 million

Source: National Statistics

More information on the 2001 Census is available from the Government Statistics website, **www.statistics.gov.uk**

Since 1951, the population has grown by 17 per cent. This is lower than the average growth for countries in the European Union (which is 23 percent), and much smaller than some other countries, such as the USA (80 per cent), and Australia (133 per cent).

Since 1951, the UK population has only grown by 17%

The UK birth rate was at an all time low in 2002 and, although it rose slightly in 2003, Britain now has an ageing population. For the first time, people aged 60 and over form a larger part of the population than children under 16. There is also a record number of people aged 85 and over.

Although there has been a general increase in population in the UK over the last 20 years, the growth has not been uniform, and some areas, such as the North East and North West of England have experienced a decline.

The Census

A census of the population in Britain has been taken every ten years since 1801 (with the exception of 1941, when Britain was at war). The next census will be in 2011.

When a census takes place, a census form is delivered to households throughout the country, and by law must be completed. The form asks for a lot of information to ensure that official statistics about the population are accurate, but is all completely confidential and anonymous as regards each individual. Only after 100 years can the records be consulted freely.

Ethnic diversity

The largest ethnic minority in Britain are people of Indian descent. These are followed by those of Pakistani descent, of mixed ethnic descent, Black Caribbean descent, Black African descent, and Bangladeshi descent. Together these groups make up 7.9 per cent of the UK population.

Today, about half the members of the African Caribbean, Pakistani, Indian, and Bangladeshi communities were born in Britain. Considerable numbers of people of Chinese, Italian, Greek and Turkish Cypriot, Polish, Australian, Canadian, New Zealand and American descent are also resident within the UK.

United Kingdom Population Ethnic Groups 2001

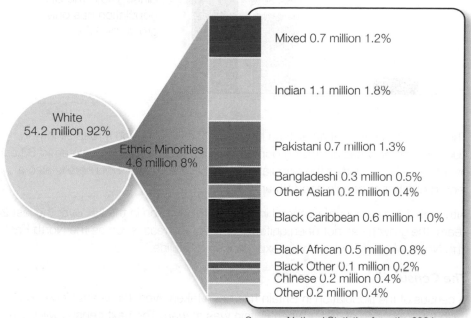

White 54.2 million 92%

Ethnic Minorities 4.6 million 8%

Mixed 0.7 million 1.2%

Indian 1.1 million 1.8%

Pakistani 0.7 million 1.3%

Bangladeshi 0.3 million 0.5%
Other Asian 0.2 million 0.4%

Black Caribbean 0.6 million 1.0%

Black African 0.5 million 0.8%

Black Other 0.1 million 0.2%
Chinese 0.2 million 0.4%
Other 0.2 million 0.4%

Source: National Statistics from the 2001 census

Where do people live?

Most members of ethnic minority groups live in England, where they make up nine per cent of the total population. This compares with two per cent each in Wales and Scotland, and less than one per cent in Northern Ireland.

45 per cent of the population of ethnic minorities live in the London area, where they comprise 29 per cent of all residents. Most other members of ethnic minorities in Britain live in one of four other areas: the West Midlands, the South East, the North West, and Yorkshire and Humberside.

REVISION QUESTIONS

Check your understanding of this unit by completing the questions below. Check your answers on page 183

28	What was the population of the United Kingdom in 2001?
	ANSWER:

29	What is the population of Northern Ireland?
	ANSWER:

30	What is the population of Wales?
	ANSWER:

31	What is the population of Scotland?
	ANSWER:

32	What is the population of England?
	ANSWER:

33	How much has the UK population grown by (in percentage terms) since 1951?
	ANSWER:

34	When will the next UK census be carried out?
	ANSWER:

35	How often is a census carried out in the United Kingdom?
	ANSWER:

36	When was the first census carried out in the United Kingdom?
	ANSWER:

37	Why was a census not carried out in the United Kingdom in 1941?
	ANSWER:

38	How many years must have passed before an individual's census form can be viewed by the public?
	ANSWER:

39	What percentage of the United Kingdom's population is made up of ethnic minorities?
	ANSWER:

40	What is the largest ethnic minority in Britain?
	ANSWER:

41	What overall proportion of today's African Caribbean, Pakistani, Indian and Bangladeshi communities in Britain were born there?
	ANSWER:

42	What percentage of the UK's ethnic minorities live in the London area?
	ANSWER:

43	What percentage of London's residents are ethnic minorities?
	ANSWER:

Religion and tolerance

Everyone in Britain has the right to religious freedom. Although Britain is historically a Christian society, people are usually very tolerant towards the faiths of others and those who have no religious beliefs.

In the 2001 Census, just over 75 per cent of the UK population reported that they had a religion. More than seven people out of ten stated that this was Christian. Nearly three per cent of the population described their religion as Muslim, and one per cent as Hindu. After these, the next largest religious groups are Sikhs, Jews, and Buddhists.

United Kingdom Population by Religion 2001

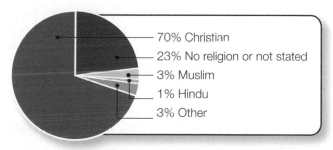

- 70% Christian
- 23% No religion or not stated
- 3% Muslim
- 1% Hindu
- 3% Other

Source: National Statistics

Although many people in Britain have a religious belief, this is not always matched by regular attendance at services. It is estimated that regular church attendance in England is between eight and eleven per cent of the population. Church attendance in Scotland however, although declining, is almost twice the level for England and Wales.

The established church

The Church of England, or Anglican Church as it is also known, came into existence in 1534. The King installed himself as head of the Church, and the title of Supreme Governor has been held by the King or Queen ever since.

The monarch at the coronation is required to swear to maintain the Protestant Religion in the United Kingdom, and heirs to the throne are not allowed to marry anyone who is not Protestant. The Queen or King also has the right to appoint a number of senior church officers, including the Archbishop of Canterbury, who is the head of the Church. In practice however, the Prime Minister makes this selection on the recommendation of a special committee appointed by the Church.

Other Christian groups

Further splits in the Church took place after the Reformation, giving rise to a number of different Protestant denominations. These included the Baptists, Presbyterians, and the Society of Friends (or Quakers), all of which continue today. In the eighteenth century the Methodist movement developed, working in particular amongst poorer members of society.

In Wales today, Baptists and Methodists are the two most widespread denominations. In Scotland there are more than a million members of the Presbyterian Church, the established Church of Scotland, known as the Kirk.

About ten per cent of the population of Britain are Roman Catholic.

The regions of Britain

Britain is a relatively small country. The distance from the north coast of Scotland to the south cost of England is approximately 600 miles (almost 1,000 km), and it is about 320 miles (just over 500 km) across the widest part of England and Wales. However, nowhere in Britain is more than 75 miles (120 km) from the coast.

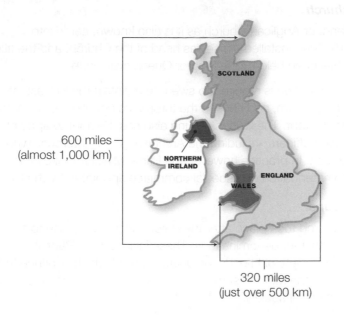

600 miles
(almost 1,000 km)

SCOTLAND

NORTHERN
IRELAND

ENGLAND

WALES

320 miles
(just over 500 km)

Many people remark on the great variety in the British landscape. In the space of a few hours it is possible to travel from a major cosmopolitan city to historic sites, old cathedrals, villages, moors and mountains.

Regional differences

In one respect, almost every part of Britain is the same. A common language, national newspapers, radio, and television, and shops with branches throughout the United Kingdom mean that everybody, to some degree, shares a similar culture. However beneath the increasingly standardised appearance of our city centres and suburbs, there are real diversities and cultural differences between different parts of the United Kingdom.

Possibly the two most distinctive areas of Britain are Wales and Scotland. Both have their own language. Welsh is taught in schools and widely spoken in north and west Wales. Gaelic is still spoken in the Highlands and Islands of Scotland. Many people believe that the Welsh and the Scots have a stronger sense of identity and culture than the English – perhaps brought about by their struggle to stay independent. The creation of the Assembly for Wales and the Scottish Parliament in 1999 has led some people to suggest that England needs its own parliament and there is now considerable discussion about what is a distinctive English identity.

Accents are a clear indication of regional differences in Britain. Geordie, Scouse, and Cockney are well known dialects from Tyneside, Liverpool, and London respectively, but other differences in speech exist in all parts of the country. Scottish and Welsh speech is distinctive, and varies within those two countries. In some areas a person's accent will indicate where they are from, within a distance of twenty miles.

Regional differences also exist in the styles of buildings and the materials used in their construction. Thatched cottages, much less common than they once were, are mainly products of the south, the south-west and east of England. Older buildings are usually made from local stone, giving houses in North Yorkshire, Derbyshire, and many other places a unique appearance.

The industrial legacy of regions also gives rise to distinct styles of architecture. The mill towns of northern England are good examples of this. The insularity of some communities, particularly on the coast and in remote corners of Britain, has meant that their appearance has changed very little in the past 50 years. In contrast, other areas, whose traditional industries have been replaced by others, are almost unrecognisable from what they were a generation ago.

REVISION QUESTIONS

Check your understanding of this unit by completing the questions below. Check your answers on page 183

44	According to the 2001 Census, what percentage of the UK population reported that they had a religion?
	ANSWER:
45	According to the 2001 Census, what percentage of people stated their religion as Muslim?
	ANSWER:
46	According to the 2001 Census, what percentage of people stated their religion as Christian?
	ANSWER:
47	Which other name is used to refer to the Church of England?
	ANSWER:
48	In what year did the Church of England come into existence?
	ANSWER:

49 What is the title of the King or Queen within the Church of England?

ANSWER:

50 What must a Monarch swear to maintain as part of their coronation?

ANSWER:

51 Who appoints the Archbishop of Canterbury?

ANSWER:

52 According to the Church of England, heirs to the throne are not allowed to marry whom?

ANSWER:

53 What is the Church of Scotland also known as?

ANSWER:

54 What percentage of the British population are Roman Catholic?

ANSWER:

55 What is the distance from the north coast of Scotland to the south coast of England?

ANSWER:

56 What is the distance of the widest part across England and Wales?

ANSWER:

57 In which year were the Assembly for Wales and the Scottish Parliament created?

ANSWER:

58 What are the two most widespread Christian denominations in Wales?

ANSWER:

59 Where is the Gaelic language spoken?

ANSWER:

60 Where is the Welsh language spoken?

ANSWER:

61 Where are Scouse dialects spoken?

ANSWER:

62	Where are Cockney dialects spoken?
	ANSWER:
63	Where are Geordie dialects spoken?
	ANSWER:

Customs and traditions

Tourist guides commonly paint a view of a rural Britain that is not always recognisable to those who live here. The countryside is regarded by many as 'real England', but in fact, the great majority of people live in cities or their suburbs. People's lives in the UK, like many others throughout the world, are a mixture of the old and the new. City dwellers love to visit the countryside. But the abolition of fox hunting, regarded by many city dwellers as long overdue, has been bitterly contested by most country dwellers who see it as a denial of their values and traditions.

Festivals and other traditions continue to exist in all parts of the country, but their existence depends almost entirely on the continued support of those who live in the local community.

Sport

Sport of all kind plays a major part in many people's lives. Football, rugby, and cricket all have a large following, and success on the sporting field is a great source of local and national pride. Major sporting events, such as the Grand National horse race, the Football Association (FA) Cup Final, and the Wimbledon tennis championships, capture the attention of many people in Britain, including those who do not normally follow these sports.

National Days

National days are not celebrated in Britain in the same way as they are in a number of other countries. Only in Northern Ireland (and the Republic of Ireland) is St Patrick's Day taken as an official holiday. The greatest celebrations are normally reserved for the New Year and the Christian festivals of Christmas and Easter.

1st March	St David's Day, the national day of Wales
17th March	St Patrick's Day, the national day of both Northern Ireland and the Republic of Ireland
23rd April	St George's Day, the national day of England
30th November	St Andrew's Day, the national day of Scotland

There are also four public holidays a year, called Bank Holidays, when legislation requires banks and most businesses to close. These are of no nationalistic or religious significance.

Religious and traditional festivals

Most religious festivals in Britain are based on the Christian tradition, but also widely recognised are customs and traditions such as Eid ul-Fitr, Divali and Yom Kippur, belonging to other religions. Many of these are explained to children in all the schools as part of their lessons in religious education; and they are celebrated by followers of these faiths in their communities.

The main Christian and traditional festivals

Christmas Day, 25th December, celebrates the birth of Jesus Christ. It is normally seen as a time to be spent at home with one's family. Preparations often begin three or four weeks beforehand, as people decide what presents to buy for close family and friends.

A Christmas tree is usually decorated and installed in the entrance hall or living room, around which presents are placed before they are opened on Christmas Day. Christmas cards are normally sent to family and friends from the beginning of December. Non-Christians usually send cards too, which will often simply say 'Seasons Greetings'. Houses are decorated with special Christmas garlands, and sometimes a wreath of holly on the front door. Mistletoe is often hung above doorways, beneath which couples should traditionally kiss. Christmas is both a religious and a secular holiday, celebrated by believers and non-believers alike. Many families attend a church service, either at midnight on Christmas Eve, or on Christmas morning.

Children hang up a long sock, stocking, or pillowcase at the foot of their bed, or around the fireplace for Father Christmas to fill with presents. On Christmas Day families traditionally sit down to a dinner of roast turkey, followed by Christmas pudding – a rich steamed pudding made from suet, dried fruit and spices.

The British Father Christmas is a cheerful old man with a beard, dressed in a red suit trimmed with fur. He travels from an area close to the North Pole on a sledge pulled by reindeer, delivering presents to children. The Father Christmas we have today is often said to be based on folklore that Dutch, German and Swedish settlers brought to America, although there are a number of other rival theories explaining his origins.

Boxing Day, 26th December, refers to a time when servants, gardeners, and other trades people used to receive money (a Christmas box) in appreciation for the work they had done throughout the year. Many people still give to postmen.

Boxing Day is a holiday in Britain, where people visit family and friends and continue with Christmas festivities. It is also a popular day for sporting activities – weather permitting.

New Year, 1st January, is celebrated in Britain, as it is in many countries throughout the world. Parties or celebrations begin on New Year's Eve, and when midnight arrives everybody cheers and drinks a toast for good luck in the coming year.

In Scotland, New Year can be a bigger festival than Christmas. Here there is a tradition in many homes of first footing, in which the first visitor of the New Year brings in particular items such as coal, bread and whisky intended to ensure prosperity for the coming year.

In Wales, on the stroke of midnight, the back door is opened to release the Old Year. It is then locked to keep the luck in, and at the last stroke, the front door opened to let in the New Year.

Easter, which takes place in March or April, commemorates the Crucifixion and Resurrection of Jesus Christ, although it is named after the Saxon goddess of spring, Eostre, whose feast took place at the Spring equinox. Easter, like Christmas, has become increasingly secular, and often taken as an opportunity for a holiday.

Easter eggs, made from chocolate (traditionally, decorated chicken's eggs) are given as presents, particularly to children, symbolising new life and the coming of spring. Some places hold festivals and fairs on Easter Monday.

Other traditions

St Valentine's Day, 14th February, is the day when boyfriends, girlfriends, husbands, and wives traditionally exchange cards and presents; cards are unsigned as if from secret admirers.

Mothering Sunday, three weeks before Easter, is a day on which children, young and old, remember their mothers by giving them flowers or chocolates and trying to make their day as easy and enjoyable as possible.

April Fool's Day, 1st April, is the day when people may play jokes on one another – but only until 12 noon. Sometimes even radio, television, and newspapers try to fool people with fake stories and jokes. The tradition is believed to have originated in sixteenth century France.

Guy Fawkes Night, 5th November, commemorates the Gunpowder Plot in 1605 when a small group of Catholics are said to have plotted to kill the King by blowing up the Houses of Parliament. Soldiers arrested Guido (Guy) Fawkes who was allegedly guarding the explosives beneath Parliament. Today he is remembered with fireworks and the burning of a 'Guy' on a bonfire.

Remembrance Day, 11th November, keeps alive the memory of those who died in both World Wars and in later conflicts. Many people now hold a two minute silence at 11.00am in remembrance of this, for it was at the eleventh hour, of the eleventh day, of the eleventh month in 1918 that the First World War (often called the Great War) finally came to an end.

The terrible fighting in the fields of Northern France and Flanders devastated the countryside and, in the disturbed earth of the bomb craters, it was the poppy that was one of the first plants to regrow. So this blood-red flower has come to symbolise the sacrifice of those who fall in war.

Today, in the period before Remembrance Day, artificial poppies are sold in shops and on the streets, and many people wear them in their buttonholes in memory of the dead.

REVISION QUESTIONS

Check your understanding of this unit by completing the questions below. Check your answers on page 184

64	Which of the UK national days is celebrated with a holiday? Name the country where this is celebrated ANSWER:
65	What and when are the national days of the four countries of the United Kingdom? ANSWER:
66	How many bank holidays are there each year in the United Kingdom? ANSWER:
67	When is Christmas and what does it celebrate? ANSWER:
68	When are Christmas presents opened? ANSWER:

69 What is mistletoe traditionally used for during Christmas?

ANSWER:

70 What is traditionally eaten on Christmas Day?

ANSWER:

71 Where does Father Christmas folklore originate?

ANSWER:

72 When is Boxing Day and what does it celebrate?

ANSWER:

73 When is New Year celebrated in the United Kingdom?

ANSWER:

74 If you were the first visitor of the new year to a Scottish home, what might you be expected to bring?

ANSWER:

75 If you were visiting a Welsh home during the new year, what tradition might be observed?

ANSWER:

76 What do Easter eggs symbolise?

ANSWER:

77 When is Easter celebrated and what does it commemorate?

ANSWER:

78 When is St Valentine's Day, and what traditionally happens that day?

ANSWER:

79 When is Mothering Sunday, and what traditionally happens that day?

ANSWER:

80 When is April Fool's Day, and what traditionally happens that day?

ANSWER:

81 When is Guy Fawkes Night and what does it commemorate?

ANSWER:

82 When is Remembrance Day and what does it commemorate?

ANSWER:

83 When did the First World War end?

ANSWER:

84 What tradition is observed in the period before Remembrance Day?

ANSWER:

UNIT 2 SUMMARY: BRITAIN TODAY: A PROFILE

In the Life in the UK Test you could be asked questions about anything included in this unit, but some of the key facts you should remember are:

- The population of the United Kingdom in 2001 was just under 59 million made up of: England 49.1 million (83%); Scotland 5.1 million (9%); Wales 2.9 million (5%); Northern Ireland 1.7 million (3%)

- Since 1951 the population of the UK has increased by 17%

- A census of the population is taken every 10 years. The next census will be in 2011

- Ethnic minorities make up 7.9% of the population, of which the largest group is Indian

- 45% of the population of ethnic minorities live in London, where they make up 29% of all residents

- 75% of the population report that they have a religion

- Seven out of ten people with a religion are Christian

- The main Christian religion is Anglican or Church of England, which is headed by the Archbishop of Canterbury

- The Anglican Church was established in 1534

- The Anglican Church is a protestant religion. Other protestant religions in Britain include Baptists, Quakers, Methodists and Presbyterians

- The Presbyterian Church is the Church of Scotland, also known as the Kirk

- About 10% of the British population are Roman Catholic

- Welsh is most commonly spoken in the north and west of Wales

- Gaelic is spoken in the Highlands and Islands of Scotland

- Regional accents in speech are common. Well known accents include Geordie (Tyneside), Scouse (Liverpool) and Cockney (London)

UNIT 3:
HOW BRITAIN IS GOVERNED

In this unit you will learn the basic elements of how government in Britain works. You need to focus on the institutions that have developed in the country, such as the roles of Prime Minister and Cabinet. Britain is unusual as it does not have a written constitution. A written constitution is, basically, a set of rules for how government must operate in a country. Britain uses a set of institutions, conventions and traditions to provide the guidance usually delivered by a written constitution. You need to think about how these different elements work together to ensure that politicians use the power they are given wisely and fairly. Also crucial to government in Britain is the role played by political parties. These groups of people and politicians, with similar ideals and values, are crucial to the outcomes of elections and to the way decisions are reached in parliament.

You may find that this unit introduces a lot of terms that are unfamiliar. If so, use the Words to Know section on page 93 to help understand the unit and to learn the terms.

HOW BRITAIN IS GOVERNED

The Working System

Parliamentary democracy

The British system of government is parliamentary democracy. General elections are held at least every five years, and voters in each constituency elect their MP (Member of Parliament) to sit in the House of Commons. Most MPs belong to a political party, and the party with the largest number of MPs in the House of Commons forms the government, with the more senior MPs becoming ministers in charge of departments of state or heads of committees of MPs.

The Prime Minister

The Prime Minister (PM) is the leader of the party in power. He or she appoints (and dismisses) ministers of state, and has the ultimate choice and control over many important public appointments. The Prime Minister's leading ministers form the Cabinet. The Prime Minister used to be called (in the lawyer's Latin of the old days) 'primus inter pares', first among equals; but nowadays the office has become so powerful that some people liken it to the French or American Presidency, an office directly elected by the people for a fixed term.

However, a Prime Minister who is defeated in an important vote in the House of Commons, or who loses the confidence of the Cabinet, can be removed by their party at any time. This rarely happens, but when it does, the event is dramatic and the effects can be great. For example, Winston Churchill replaced Prime Minister Neville Chamberlain in 1940; and Margaret Thatcher was forced to resign in 1990, when she lost the confidence of her colleagues.

Modern Prime Ministers have their official residence at 10 Downing Street, and have a considerable staff of civil servants and personal advisers. The PM has special advisers for publicity and relations with the press and broadcasting media – all of which adds to the power of the Prime Minister over his or her colleagues. Government statements are usually reported as coming from 'Number Ten'. If something is directly attributed to the Prime Minister it is of special importance.

The Cabinet

The Cabinet is a small committee of about twenty senior politicians who normally meet weekly to decide the general policies for the Government. Amongst those included in the Cabinet are ministers responsible for the economy (the Chancellor of the Exchequer), law and order and immigration (the Home Secretary), foreign affairs (the Foreign Secretary), education, health, and defence. Cabinet decisions on major matters of policy and law are submitted to Parliament for approval.

The British constitution

To say that a state has a constitution can mean two different things in different countries. Usually it means a set of written rules governing how laws can be made, and setting out the rights and duties of citizens that can be enforced by a constitutional or supreme court. But sometimes there is no written constitution so that the term simply describes how a state is governed, what are the main institutions of government and the usual conventions observed by the government and the politicians.

The United Kingdom constitution is an unwritten constitution. But although no laws passed by Parliament can be directly challenged by any British court, there are restraints on government. Laws define the maximum length of parliaments, the electoral system, qualifications for citizenship, and the rights of non-citizens. There are the rules and procedures of Parliament itself, and interpretations of laws made by the courts in light of the traditions of the common law.

Sovereignty

A fundamental principle of the British constitution is 'the sovereignty of Parliament'. But nowadays decisions of the European Union have to be observed because of the treaties that Britain has entered into; and British courts must observe the judgements of the European Court and the new Human Rights Act. Textbooks are written on 'The British Constitution' and constitutional law, but no one authority will agree fully with another. Some constitutional disputes are highly political – such as what should be the composition and powers of the House of Lords and what is the best system of national and local elections.

Some reformers want a written constitution, as does the third largest party at Westminster, the Liberal-Democrats. But others, including the leaders of the Labour and Conservative parties, value historical continuity coupled with flexibility and have no wish for big issues to be settled by a constitutional court, as in the United States and many other democratic countries. But what holds the unwritten system together is that party leaders observe conventions of political conduct.

Conventions

Conventions and traditions are very important in British political life. For example, the second largest party in the House of Commons not merely opposes the Government but is called 'Her Majesty's Loyal Opposition'. It has a guaranteed amount of time in Parliament to debate matters of its own choice, and its rights are defended by the Speaker, who chairs proceedings in the House of Commons.

The Leader of the Opposition has offices in Parliament and receives financial support from the Treasury both for his or her office and for the Shadow Cabinet. These are senior members of the main opposition party who 'shadow' Government ministers in different departments. The Leader of the Opposition also has a constitutional status (that is why we use capital letters). He or she stands beside the Prime Minister on formal state occasions, as when the Queen opens Parliament or when wreaths are laid at the Cenotaph in Whitehall on Remembrance Day.

Question Time, when Members of Parliament may ask questions of government ministers, is another parliamentary convention. Questions to the Prime Minister by the Leader of the Opposition are usually lively and combative occasions, often widely reported.

British Parliament

House of Lords	House of Commons	
	Governing Party	**Opposition & other non-governing parties**
Hereditary Peers	Prime Minister	Leader of the Opposition
Life Peers	Ministers & members of the Cabinet	Shadow Ministers
Senior Bishops & Judges	Whips	Whips
	Other MPs associated with the governing party	Other MPs not associated with the governing party

A competitive party system

Under the British system of parliamentary democracy, candidates nominated by political parties, and sometimes individual independent candidates, compete for the votes of the electorate in general elections and by-elections. (By-elections are held to fill a vacancy when an MP resigns or dies in office). The struggle between the parties to influence public opinion, however, is continuous, and takes place not only at election time.

The role of the media

Proceedings in Parliament are now broadcast on digital television and recorded in official reports, known as Hansard. Although copies of this are available in large libraries and on the Internet, **www.parliament.uk**, most people receive their information about political issues and events from newspapers, TV and radio.

In Britain there is a free press – that is, one that is free from direct government control. The owners and editors of most newspapers hold strong political opinions and run campaigns to influence government policy. All newspapers have their own angle in reporting and commenting on political events. Sometimes it is difficult to distinguish fact from opinion. Spokesmen and women of all political parties put their own slant on things too – known today as 'spin'.

In Britain, the law states that political reporting on radio and television must be balanced. In practice, this means giving equal time to rival viewpoints. Broadcasters are free to interview politicians in a tough and lively fashion, as long as their opponents are also interviewed and treated in more or less the same way.

During a general election, the main parties are given free time on radio and television to make short party political broadcasts. In citizenship lessons in schools young people are encouraged to read newspapers critically and to follow news and current affairs programmes on radio and television.

REVISION QUESTIONS

Check your understanding of this unit by completing the questions below. Check your answers on page 185

85	How often are general elections held in the UK?
	ANSWER:
86	What is MP short for?
	ANSWER:
87	What is the role of the Prime Minister?
	ANSWER:
88	What did the Prime Minister used to be called in Latin?
	ANSWER:
89	Where are government statements usually reported as coming from?
	ANSWER:
90	What is the name of the ministerial position that is responsible for the economy?
	ANSWER:
91	What is the name of the ministerial position that is responsible for order and immigration?
	ANSWER:

92 What happens to policy & law decisions once they have been agreed by Cabinet?

ANSWER:

93 What is the name of the ministerial position that is responsible for foreign affairs?

ANSWER:

94 Where is the Prime Minister's official residence?

ANSWER:

95 Approximately how many MPs are there in Cabinet?

ANSWER:

96 What is the Cabinet?

ANSWER:

97 How is it decided which party forms the Government?

ANSWER:

98 What type of constitution does the UK have?

ANSWER:

99 What is the second largest party in the House of Commons called by convention?

ANSWER:

100 What is the role of the Speaker in the House of Commons?

ANSWER:

101 What happens during Question Time?

ANSWER:

102 When are by-elections held?

ANSWER:

103 Can newspapers publish opinions and run campaigns to influence government?

ANSWER:

104 What is the name of the official reports of proceedings in Parliament?

ANSWER:

105 What laws exist regarding political reporting on radio and television?
ANSWER:

UNIT 3 SUMMARY: THE WORKING SYSTEM

In the Life in the UK Test you could be asked questions about anything included in this unit, but some of the key facts you should remember are:

- Britain is a parliamentary democracy. This means that representatives are regularly elected to a national parliament

- General elections are held at least every five years, when voters in each constituency elect their own representative to sit in the House of Commons

- The political party that wins the most constituencies receives the right to form the Government

- The Prime Minister is the leader of the party that forms the Government. The Prime Minister has many powers, including the right to make many important appointments

- The Prime Minister has their official residence at 10 Downing Street

- The Prime Minister has been known as primus inter pares or first among equals

- The Cabinet is a committee of about 20 senior politicians from the party in power. Its members are appointed by the Prime Minister

- Britain does not have a written constitution. Instead the country is governed using various rules for politicians and people in positions of influence

- The second largest party in parliament is known as 'Her Majesty's Loyal Opposition'. The Leader of the Opposition operates in direct competition to the Prime Minister and is supported by the Shadow Cabinet

- Question Time is a regular session of parliament when Ministers answer questions posed by MPs

- All proceedings in parliament are recorded in official reports, called Hansard

- Britain has a free press. This means that the government has no direct control over the press. Individual newspapers and other media organisations usually have their own view on political events

- The law requires that political reporting on television and radio is balanced. This means that different viewpoints must be given equal time

- Before a general election the main political parties are given free time to make party political broadcasts on television and radio

UNIT 4:
THE FORMAL INSTITUTIONS

In this unit you will learn about the permanent institutions that make up the foundations of politics and government in Britain. In the previous unit you learnt that Britain does not have a formal constitution and is instead governed using a number of unwritten rules and practices. This unit focuses in more depth on the operation of those institutions that allow government in Britain to operate without a written constitution. These institutions work together to provide fair and good government, but they also act as checks, sometimes working against each other, to make sure that unfair decisions are not made. You need to focus on each individual institution and how it operates.

THE FORMAL INSTITUTIONS

Government and politics in Britain takes place in the context of mainly traditional institutions, law and conventions, which ensure the acceptance of electoral or Parliamentary defeat, and peaceful and reasonably tolerant behaviour between political rivals.

The institutional arrangements are a constitutional monarchy, the House of Commons, the House of Lords, the electoral system, the party system and pressure groups, the judiciary, the police, the civil service, local government, and the recent devolved administrations of Scotland, Wales and Northern Ireland, together with a large number of semi-independent agencies set up by the government, nicknamed quangos, and now officially called Non Departmental Public Bodies.

A Constitutional Monarchy

Britain has a constitutional monarchy. Others exist in Denmark, Netherlands, Norway, Spain, and Sweden. Under a constitutional monarchy, the powers of the King or Queen are limited by either constitutional law or convention.

In Britain, the Queen or King must accept the decisions of the Cabinet and Parliament. The monarch can express her or his views on government matters privately to the Prime Minister, for example at their weekly 'audience', but in all matters of government must follow the Prime Minister's advice. The Queen or King can only, in a famous phrase, 'advise, warn, and encourage'. There would be a constitutional crisis if the monarch ever spoke out publicly either for or against government policy.

The present Queen has reigned since her father's death in 1952. The heir to the throne is her oldest son, the Prince of Wales. He has let his opinions be publicly known on a range of environmental and other matters, but when he becomes King he will be required to act and speak only in a ceremonial manner. Today there are some who argue that modern Britain should become a republic, with an elected President. However, despite public criticisms of some members of the royal family, the monarchy still remains important and popular among most people in Britain today as a symbol of national unity. People distinguish between the persons of the royal family and the institutions they represent.

The Queen is Head of State of the United Kingdom. She is also monarch or head of state, in both a ceremonial and symbolic sense, of most of the countries in the Commonwealth. The Queen has important ceremonial roles in this country, which include the opening and closing of Parliament. Each year at the beginning of a new parliamentary session she reads by tradition 'the Queen's speech' from a throne in the House of Lords, stating the Government's policies for the next session. Today however, these are entirely the views of the Prime Minister and the cabinet.

The monarch also gives the letters of appointment to holders of high office within the Government, the armed forces, and the Church of England, but always on the Prime Minister's advice.

The House of Commons

The House of Commons is the centre of political debate in Britain and the ultimate source of power. It shares the huge Palace of Westminster with the House of Lords. In medieval times, the House of Lords was the more powerful, and so you will still hear some commentators call the Commons, the Lower House, and the Lords, the Upper House. Today the Commons can always overrule the Lords who can only delay the passage of new laws.

The MPs who sit in the House of Commons are elected from 645 constituencies throughout the UK. They have a number of different responsibilities. They represent everyone in their constituency, they help create and shape new laws, they scrutinise and comment on what the Government is doing, and they provide a forum for debate on important national issues. If you visit the House of Commons you may find few MPs in the main debating chamber. That is because most work is done in committees – scrutinising legislation, investigating administration, or preparing a report on some important issue.

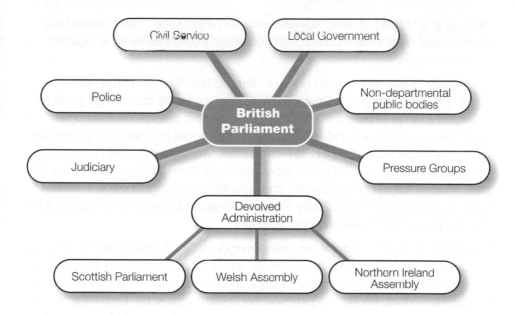

Visiting parliament

There are public galleries from which the public may listen to debates in both Houses of Parliament and many committees. You can write to your local MP to ask for tickets. There is no charge, but MPs only have a small allocation of tickets, so requests should be made well in advance. Otherwise, on the day, you can join a queue at the public entrance, but a waiting time of one or two hours is common for important debates. Getting into the House of Lords is usually easier. Ask the police officer at the same entrance where to go. Further details are on the UK Parliament website, **www.parliament.uk**

The Speaker

The Speaker of the House of Commons is an ordinary MP, respected on all sides, and elected by fellow MPs. He or she has the important role of keeping order during political debates in a fair and impartial way; of representing the House of Commons on ceremonial occasions; and of ensuring the smooth running of the business of the House.

The Whips

The Whips are small groups of MPs, appointed by their party leaders, to ensure discipline and attendance of MPs at voting time in the House of Commons. The Chief Whip commonly attends Cabinet or Shadow Cabinet meetings and will negotiate with the Speaker over the timetable and the order of business.

The House of Lords

The House of Lords is in the middle of big changes. Until relatively recently, the members were all peers of the realm; that is hereditary aristocrats, or people who had been rewarded for their public service – for example in war, the Empire or government. They had no special duty to attend the House of Lords, and many did not do so.

In 1957 a new law was passed, enabling the Prime Minister to appoint peers just for their own lifetime. These Life Peers, as they were known, were to be working peers, and were encouraged to attend debates in the House of Lords on a regular basis. Today those appointed as life peers have normally had a distinguished career in politics, business, law or some other profession. Recently hereditary peers had their general right to attend the House of Lords removed, but were allowed to elect a small number of themselves to continue to attend.

Life peers continue to be appointed by the Prime Minister although, by convention, always include people nominated by the leaders of the other parties. Senior Bishops of the Church of England are automatically members of the House of Lords, as are most senior judges. Life peers also include members of other Christian denominations and of other faiths – Jewish, Muslim, Hindu, Sikh, or Buddhist, as well non-believers and humanists. Today the main role of the House of Lords is to examine in detail and at greater leisure new laws proposed by the House of Commons, and to suggest amendments or changes. In this way the Lords may delay – but not prevent – the passage of new legislation.

The House of Lords also frequently debates issues which the Commons pass over or can find no time for. House of Lords' committees also, from time to time, report on a particular social problem or scrutinise some aspect of the workings of government.

To prevent a government from staying in power without holding an election, the House of Lords has the absolute right to reject any proposed law that would extend the life of a Parliament beyond the statutory five year period. However, if this were ever to happen, the House of Commons could first abolish the House of Lords, who could only delay such an act! This is very unlikely but illustrates how constitutional restraints in the United Kingdom depends more on conventions than on strict law.

The Electoral System

Members of the House of Commons (MPs) are elected by a 'first past the post' system. The candidate in a constituency who gains more votes than any other is elected, even if he or she does not have a majority of the total votes cast. In the House of Commons, the government is formed by the party gaining the majority of the seats, even if more votes were cast in total for the Opposition.

Under this system, the number of seats going to the winner is always proportionately greater than their total vote. For this reason, some people argue that the system should be changed to one or other form of proportional representation, as in Ireland and most parts of continental Europe. However, neither of the main UK parties favours this, saying that large majorities in the House of Commons guarantee strong and stable government, and that PR (proportional representation) would lead to coalitions and instability.

However, the Scottish Parliament and the Welsh Assembly were both set up with different systems of PR to ensure that they were not completely dominated by a single party, as can happen under a 'first past the post' system. Similarly, the use of PR for elections to the Northern Ireland Assembly is intended to stop the Unionist (many Protestant) majority of voters from taking all the posts of government, and ensure 'power sharing' with the Irish nationalist (overwhelmingly Catholic) parties. In elections for the European Parliament yet another form of PR was adopted to conform more closely to European Union practice.

REVISION QUESTIONS

Check your understanding of this unit by completing the questions below. Check your answers on page 186

106	What are quangos?
	ANSWER:
107	What famous phrase describes the level of expression that the Monarch is restricted to when discussing government matters?
	ANSWER:
108	In which year did Queen Elizabeth II start her reign?
	ANSWER:
109	Who is the current heir to the throne?
	ANSWER:
110	Who is the Head of State of the United Kingdom?
	ANSWER:

111 What is contained in the Queen's speech?

ANSWER:

112 What ceremonial duties does the Monarch perform in the British Parliament?

ANSWER:

113 Who does the Monarch give letters of appointment to at the opening of parliament?

ANSWER:

114 The House of Commons is located in which building?

ANSWER:

115 What other names have been used to describe the House of Commons and the House of Lords?

ANSWER:

116 How many constituencies are there throughout the United Kingdom?

ANSWER:

117 What are the responsibilities of an MP?

ANSWER:

118 How can you visit Parliament?

ANSWER:

119 How is the Speaker of the House of Commons chosen?

ANSWER:

120 Who are the Whips and what do they do?

ANSWER:

121 In the past, what was the only way that members could be appointed to the House of Lords?

ANSWER:

122 In what year did the Prime Minister gain powers to be able to appoint members of the House of Lords?

ANSWER:

123	What is a Life Peer?
	ANSWER:
124	What is the main role of the House of Lords?
	ANSWER:
125	What is the name of the system that governs how MPs are elected into the House of Commons?
	ANSWER:
126	What must a party candidate achieve in order to win their constituency?
	ANSWER:
127	Where is proportional representation used in UK politics?
	ANSWER:

The Party System and Pressure Groups

The British political system is essentially a party system in the way that decisions are made and elections conducted. There is only a handful of independent MPs or MPs from smaller parties. The main political parties have membership branches in every constituency throughout Britain. Local party organisations select candidates, discuss policy, and canvas the voters in national, local and European elections. Annual national party conferences are carefully managed and well publicised events, where general party policy is debated, and where local parties can have a significant effect on the Parliamentary leadership.

Public opinion polls have also become very important to the leadership of each party. Party leaders know that they have to persuade and carry large numbers of the electorate, who are not party members, and who in recent years have become less fixed and predictable in their voting habits.

Political party membership in Britain has been declining rapidly in the last few years, perhaps as a consequence of greater consensus between the parties on the main questions of economic management, both seeking the middle ground so that differences of policy and principle are more difficult to perceive; or perhaps because people now, working longer hours and harder, and enjoying for the most part a greater standard of living, can or will give less time to public service. No one knows if this is a temporary or a long-term change. This, combined with falling turn-out in elections, especially among 18–25 year olds, has become a matter of general concern and is widely discussed in the press and in the broadcasting media.

Pressure Groups

Pressure groups are organisations that try to influence government policy, either directly or indirectly. There are many such groups in Britain today, and they are an increasingly important part of political life. Generally speaking, ordinary citizens today are more likely to support pressure groups than join a political party. Sometimes people distinguish between 'pressure groups' and 'lobbies'. Lobbies or 'interest groups' are seen not as voluntary bodies of ordinary citizens but as the voice of commercial, financial, industrial, trade, or professional organisations.

The Judiciary

Since medieval times, judges have prided themselves on being independent of the Crown. Under the British system, judges can never challenge the legality of laws passed by Parliament, but they do interpret legislation and if a law contravenes our human rights, judges can declare it incompatible. The law must then be changed.

As a rule, judges in court normally apply the law in the same way as they have done in the past. This ensures that similar cases are dealt with in a consistent way. However there are times when the circumstances of a case have not arisen before, or when senior judges decide that existing judgements do not reflect modern society. In these situations, by their decisions, judges can create or change the law.

Judges in Britain are appointed by a Government minister, the Lord Chancellor, from nominations put forward by existing judges. The names proposed are those of senior lawyers who are believed to have the ability and judgement to do the job. In the last few years however, there have been demands – to which the government is responding – that this process should become more transparent, and clearer to members of the press and public. It is also felt that judges should be more representative of the public at large. Many argue that the judges are drawn from too narrow a section of society and that women and members of ethnic minorities are not sufficiently represented.

The Police

The police are organised on a local basis, usually with one force for each county. The largest force is the Metropolitan Police, with its headquarters at New Scotland Yard, which serves London. The police have 'operational independence' – the Government cannot instruct them to arrest or proceed against any individual. But their administration is controlled by police authorities of elected local councillors and magistrates, and by the role of the Home Secretary. An independent authority investigates serious complaints against the police.

The Civil Service

The Government is serviced by a large number of independent managers and administrators, who have the job of carrying out Government policy. They are also known as civil servants.

The key features of the civil service are political neutrality and professionalism. Before the mid-nineteenth century civil servants were appointed by ministers and had to be supporters of the party in power. Civil service reform began in the early 19th century, when the East India Company governed India. To prevent corruption and favouritism, candidates were required to pass competitive examinations. In the 1860s this system was extended to the Home Civil Service and continues with many modifications today.

Members of the British civil service today are permanent servants of the state, working for whatever party is in power. This neutrality is very important, but is sometimes a difficult balance to strike. Civil servants must warn ministers if they think a policy is impractical or even against the public interest; but must ultimately find a way of putting into practice the policies of the elected Government.

Political party officials tend to do everything they can to put Government policy in a favourable light. Civil servants may find themselves in a dilemma if they think that a minister is being too optimistic about the outcome of a particular policy, or asking them to do things specifically to discredit the Opposition. In the past, commentators suspected that civil servants too easily imposed their departmental policies on new ministers; but now the suspicion is often that civil servants can on occasion be pushed into open support for party policies they think to be either impractical or incompatible with other policies.

A major restraint on civil servants from becoming too politically involved is the knowledge that, if a general election brings another party to power, they will have to work with a new Government – and an entirely different set of aims and policies. When a General Election is pending or taking place, top civil servants study closely the Opposition's policies so that they are ready to serve a new government loyally.

Local Government

Towns, cities, and rural areas in Britain are administered by a system of local government or councils, usually referred to as local authorities. Many areas have both district and county councils, although large towns and cities tend to be administered by a single authority, called a borough, metropolitan district, or city council.

Local authorities are responsible for providing a range of community services in their area – such as education, planning, environmental health, passenger transport, the fire service, social services, refuse collection, libraries, and housing. Today local authorities in England and Wales have considerably less control over the organisation of these services than they did in the past.

What local government is required to do is called 'mandatory services', as decided by central government. Citizens can take them to court if they do not perform them: But there are also 'permissive services', though less than in the past; what they may do if they want to and can afford to do. In England and Wales local authorities may only offer permissive services if empowered to do so by government legislation. However in Scotland, under devolution, local authorities can do anything they are not explicitly forbidden to do. This is a simpler system to understand and operate, but financial constraints make the two systems more similar than might be supposed.

Most of the money for local authority services comes from the Government, provided through taxation. Only about 20 per cent is funded locally through the collection of council tax. There are strict systems of accountability, which determine how local authorities spend their money, and the Government is now beginning to explore how much some local services can be delivered by voluntary community groups. Some see this as diminishing the powers of local government but others see it as a way of involving more ordinary citizens in how their area is run.

Elections for local government councillors are held in May each year. Many – but not all – candidates stand as members of a political party. A few cities in Britain, including London, also have their own elected mayors, with increased powers to manage local affairs. Serving on the local council is still frequently the first step (but less so than in the past) to getting the local party to nominate someone as a candidate for election to the national Parliament or Assembly or to the European Parliament in Strasbourg.

REVISION QUESTIONS

Check your understanding of this unit by completing the questions below. Check your answers on page 186

128 What is the distinction between a pressure group and a lobby group?

ANSWER:

129 Can a judge challenge the legality of a law?

ANSWER:

130 How are judges appointed?

ANSWER:

131 What is the name of the largest police force in the United Kingdom?

ANSWER:

132 Where are the headquarters of the Metropolitan Police force?

ANSWER:

133 Who controls the administration of the police?

ANSWER:

134 How are the police structured and organised?

ANSWER:

135 What is a civil servant?

ANSWER:

136 What are the two key features of the civil service?

ANSWER:

137 When was the civil service reformed to prevent favouritism and corruption?

ANSWER:

138 What responsibilities do local authorities have?

ANSWER:

139 Where do local authority services get most of their funding from?

ANSWER:

140 When are local government elections held?

ANSWER:

UNIT 4 SUMMARY: THE FORMAL INSTITUTIONS

In the Life in the UK Test you could be asked questions about anything included in this unit, but some of the key facts you should remember are:

- Britain has a constitutional monarchy. This means that the King or Queen has ultimate authority in the country, but in practice this authority is limited by various rules and practices

- The King or Queen must accept the decisions of the Cabinet and Parliament. He or she can only 'advise, warn and encourage'

- The present Queen has reigned since 1952

- The United Kingdom has two houses of parliament: the House of Commons and the House of Lords

- The House of Commons is where most political debate occurs and is the more powerful of the two houses of parliament

- The Members of Parliament, who sit in the House of Commons, are elected from 645 constituencies throughout the United Kingdom

- The public can visit and observe both houses of parliament and also the various committees in which politicians work

- The Speaker of the House of Commons is an ordinary Member of Parliament, respected on all sides, and elected by other Members

- The Whips are small groups of Members of Parliament who ensure discipline and attendance of other Members at important votes in the House of Commons

- The main role of the House of Lords is to examine in detail new laws proposed by the House of Commons

- In 1957 a new law was passed that allowed the Prime Minister to appoint members of the House of Lords. Before that all members were hereditary aristocrats or people who had received their position as reward for public service

- Senior Bishops of the Anglican Church, and most senior judges, automatically become members of the House of Lords

- Members of the House of Commons are elected using a 'first past the post' system. The candidate with the most votes, in each constituency, is elected

- In both the Welsh Assembly and the Scottish Parliament forms of proportional representation are used to elect members

- Judges in Britain are appointed by the Lord Chancellor from nominations put forward by existing judges

- The police are organised on a local basis, usually with one force for each county

- The largest police force in the country is the Metropolitan Police. It serves London and has its headquarters at New Scotland Yard

- Members of the civil service are permanent government employees and must work for the political party that is in power

- Local government authorities are required, by central government, to deliver mandatory services. If they choose, they may also deliver permissive services

- Elections for local government are held in May each year

UNIT 5:
DEVOLVED ADMINISTRATION

In this unit you will learn about some of the ways in which the government has passed some its powers down to other institutions. This is commonly referred to as devolved administration. Governments have chosen to do this for various reasons including giving local people more say in local issues, allowing the government to generate income or creating agencies that have clear independence from the rest of government. Perhaps the most important development in recent times has been the establishment of representative assemblies in Wales and Scotland. These national parliaments give the people of Wales and Scotland more say in how their area of the country is run. While developments in Wales and Scotland have been relatively uncontroversial, events in Northern Ireland have been some of the most troubled in recent British history. Ensure that you understand who the important groups are in the conflict in Northern Ireland. On one side you have mainly Protestant groups who want to remain tied to the United Kingdom; on the other side you have mainly Catholic groups whose allegiance lies with the Republic of Ireland. Also be sure to familiarise yourself with the different types of non-departmental bodies that exist.

DEVOLVED ADMINISTRATION

In 1997, the Government began a programme of devolving power from central government, with the intention of giving people in Wales and Scotland greater control over matters that directly affect them. Since 1999 there has been an Assembly in Wales, and a Parliament in Scotland, and the Government is now proposing the idea of regional governments in England where there is a clear local demand.

However, policy and laws governing defence, foreign affairs, taxation, and social security remain under the control of the UK Government in London, although these issues may be debated in the Welsh Assembly and the Scottish Parliament.

The National Assembly for Wales

The National Assembly for Wales is situated in Cardiff. It has 60 Assembly Members (AMs) and elections are held every four years. Members can speak in either English or Welsh and all its publications are in both languages. The Assembly does not have the power to make separate laws for Wales but it may propose laws for the decision of the UK Parliament in Westminster. However, it does have the power to decide on many other important matters, such as education policy, the environment, health services, transport and local government, where the present laws allow Welsh ministers a great deal of discretion in making detailed regulations.

The Parliament of Scotland

The Parliament of Scotland in Edinburgh arose as the result of a long campaign by people in Scotland for more independence and democratic control. For a long time there had been a devolved administration run by the Scottish Office, but no national elected body. A referendum for a Scottish Parliament, in 1979, did not gain enough support, but when another was held in 1997, the electorate gave a clear 'yes' both to establishing a Scottish Parliament and to it having limited powers to vary national income tax.

Today there are 129 Members of the Scottish Parliament (MSPs) in Edinburgh, who are elected by a form of proportional representation. Unlike the Welsh Assembly, the Scottish Parliament may pass legislation on anything not specifically reserved to Westminster (foreign affairs, defence, general economic policy, and social security).

The Scottish Parliament is funded by a grant from the UK Government and can spend it how it chooses. It has the legal power to make small changes in the lower base rate of income tax, which it has not exercised so far, and has adopted its own procedures for debate, the passage of legislation and access to the public – all deliberately different from the traditional ways of Westminster.

The Northern Ireland Assembly

The Northern Ireland Parliament, often called Stormont after the building where it met, was established in 1922, following the division of Ireland after civil war. Protestant political parties, however, dominated the Parliament, and abolished the electoral system of proportional representation that was designed to protect the Catholic minority – a community who faced considerable discrimination in housing and jobs in the public services.

The Government in London paid little attention to these problems until, 50 years later, protests, riots, and a civil disobedience campaign led them to abolish

Stormont when reforms failed to materialise. Conflicts increased between Protestant and Catholic groups, the former determined to remain part of the United Kingdom; while the latter determined to achieve unity with the Irish Republic.

There followed many years of communal distrust, violence, and terrorism. But after a negotiated cease-fire by both the main para-military groups – the IRA (the Irish Republican Army), and the UDA (the Ulster Defence Associate) – the Good Friday Agreement was signed in 1998 between the main parties and endorsed by the Irish and British governments, working closely together.

Shortly afterwards, the Northern Ireland Assembly was established, with a power-sharing agreement in which the main parties divided the ministerial offices between them. The Assembly has 108 elected members, with powers to decide on matters such as education, agriculture, environment, health, and social services in Northern Ireland.

In view of the political situation in Northern Ireland, the UK government kept the power to suspend the Assembly if the political leaders could no longer agree to work together or if the Assembly was not working in the interests of the people of Northern Ireland. This has happened on a number of occasions.

Non-departmental public bodies

Much of government that affects us all is conducted not directly, but through a multitude of agencies with various degrees of independence. These are organisations that Parliament can create or abolish, or change their powers and roles, but are not a direct part of the civil service. They are sometimes called quangos – quasi-autonomous non-governmental organisations.

A few examples of non-departmental public bodies

Trading bodies set up by central government that raise revenue:
Her Majesty's Stationery Office (official and semi-official publications), Forestry Commission, National Savings Bank, Crown Estates Commission.

Spending agencies funded by government: Regional Health Authorities, Higher Education Funding Councils, Sports Council, Arts Council, Legal Services Commission, Medical Research Council.

Quasi-judicial and prosecuting bodies: Competition Commission (previously known as the Monopolies and Mergers Commission), Criminal Injuries Compensation Authority, Police Complaints Authority, Crown Prosecution Service.

Statutory Advisory Bodies to Ministers: Gaming Board, Health and Safety Commission, Law Commission, Commission for Racial Equality, Equal

Opportunities Commission, Advisory Board on Naturalisation and Integration.

Development agencies (many of which are public-private partnerships): Scottish Enterprise, Highlands and Islands Development Board (Scotland), Welsh Development Agency, Rural Development Commission, several regional Urban Development Corporations.

REVISION QUESTIONS

Check your understanding of this unit by completing the questions below. Check your answers on page 187

141	When did the government start a programme of devolved administration for Wales and Scotland? ANSWER:
142	Which areas of policy always remain under the control of the central UK government? ANSWER:
143	Where is the National Assembly for Wales situated? ANSWER:
144	How many Assembly Members are there in the National Assembly for Wales? ANSWER:
145	When was the first referendum held for a Scottish Parliament? ANSWER:
146	When was the second referendum held for a Scottish Parliament? ANSWER:
147	How many Members of the Scottish Parliament are there? ANSWER:
148	What are the differences in power between the Welsh Assembly and the Scottish Parliament? ANSWER:
149	What is the Northern Ireland Assembly often called? ANSWER:

150	When was the Northern Ireland Parliament established?
	ANSWER:

151	When was the Good Friday Agreement signed?
	ANSWER:

152	How many members are there in the Northern Ireland Assembly?
	ANSWER:

UNIT 5 SUMMARY: DEVOLVED ADMINISTRATION

In the Life in the UK Test you could be asked questions about anything included in this unit, but some of the key facts you should remember are:

- The National Assembly for Wales and the Scottish Parliament were established in 1999

- The National Assembly for Wales, which is situated in Cardiff, has 60 Assembly Members (AMs). Elections are held every four years

- The Scottish Parliament, which is situated in Edinburgh, has 129 Members of the Scottish Parliament (MSPs)

- The Northern Ireland Parliament, also known as Stormont, was first established in 1922

- Stormont was abolished 50 years later by the UK government after a campaign of protest, riots and civil disobedience

- During an extended period of distrust, violence and terrorism in Northern Ireland the main para-military groups involved were the Irish Republican Army (IRA) and the Ulster Defence Associate (UDA)

- The Good Friday Agreement was negotiated in 1998 to bring peace to Northern Ireland

- The Northern Ireland Assembly was established shortly after the Good Friday Agreement was negotiated. It has 108 members and shares ministerial responsibility between the main parties

- The government is able to set up non-departmental public bodies. These bodies have a degree of independence from the rest of government. They are sometimes called quangos – quasi-autonomous non-governmental organisations

UNIT 6:
BRITAIN IN EUROPE
AND THE WORLD

In this unit you will learn about the position that Britain has in the continent of Europe and in the world as a whole. The most important factor you need to understand is how much Britain has changed as it relates to the rest of the world. The power that Britain had in the world reduced massively during the twentieth century as the British Empire gradually dissolved. This has meant that other countries now have a very different view of Britain, and at the same time Britain also sees the rest of the world very differently. Central to these changes is the role of the Second World War. While Britain and its Allies were victorious in the war, Britain's economy and its influence in the world was left heavily damaged. Britain has gradually moved into closer cooperation with its European neighbours and is now a key member of the European Union. Make sure you understand the crucial role that the European Union has in British government, law, politics and the economy. At the same time as Britain has strengthened its association with Europe its ties to former members of the British Empire have reduced, but the emergence of the Commonwealth means that these ties have not been completely lost.

BRITAIN IN EUROPE AND THE WORLD

In addition to Britain's historical and cultural ties with countries throughout Europe, two major developments have occurred since the end of the Second World War in 1945 closely linking Britain to the remainder of Europe.

Europe

The Council of Europe

The Council of Europe was created in 1949, and Britain was one of the founder members. It is an organisation with 50 member states, working to protect human rights and seek solutions to problems facing European society today. The Council of Europe has no power to make laws, but does draw up conventions and charters, which member states agree to follow. Examples of these are the European Convention on Human Rights, measures to trace the assets associated with organised crime, and a directive for education for democratic citizenship in schools.

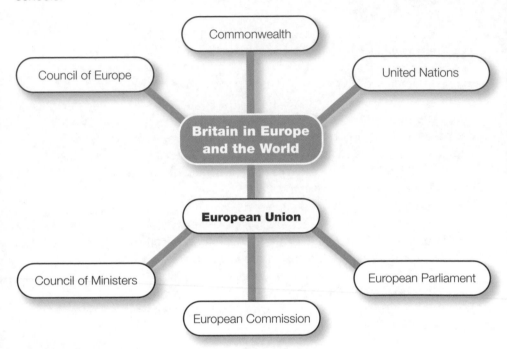

The European Union

The European Union originated in the period immediately after the Second World War when Belgium, France, Luxembourg, the Netherlands, and West Germany signed an agreement putting all their coal and steel production under the control of a single authority. An important reason for doing this was the belief that co-operation between these states would reduce the likelihood of another European war.

Britain refused to join this group at the beginning and only became part of the European Union (or European Economic Community, as it was then known) in 1973 after twice being vetoed by France. In 2004, ten new member countries joined the EU bringing membership to a total of 25.

The main aim behind the European Union today is for member states to become a single market. To achieve this, measures have gradually been introduced to remove tariff barriers and to help people, goods, and services move freely and easily between member states. This has involved a great deal of regulation being imposed on businesses and consumers, and has not always been popular.

Citizens of a EU member state have the right to travel to any EU country as long as they have a valid passport or identity card. This right may be restricted only for reasons of public health, public order, or public security. They also have the right to work in other EU countries, and must be offered employment under the same conditions as citizens of that state.

The Council of Ministers

The Council of Ministers is one of the most influential bodies in the EU. It is made up of government ministers meeting periodically from each member state with powers to propose new laws and take important decisions about how the EU is run.

The European Commission

Based in Brussels, the European Commission is rather like the civil service of the European Union, taking care of the day to day running of the organisation. One of the important jobs the European Commission is to draft proposals for new EU policies and law.

The European Parliament

The European Parliament meets in Strasbourg in north-eastern France. Each country elects members roughly proportional to its population. Elections for Members of the European Parliament (MEPs) are held every five years.

The Parliament scrutinises and debates the proposals, decisions, and expenditures of the Commission, but does not decide policy. MEPs have the ultimate power to refuse to agree EU expenditure, but have never done so – although they have held it up. Yet the threat has proved effective on several occasions.

European Union law

European Union law is an important source of law in Britain. EU legislation consists mainly of Regulations and Directives. Regulations are specific rules, such as those limiting the hours that drivers of goods vehicles can work, which automatically have the force of law in all EU member states. Regulations override national legislation and must be followed by the courts in each member state.

Directives are general requirements that must be introduced within a set time, but the way in which they are implemented is left to each member state. An example of this is the procedures that must be followed by companies when making staff redundant.

All proposals for new EU laws are examined by a committee of the UK Parliament, which then recommends any changes or amendments to ministers, who will decide whether to try and change or renegotiate them.

The World

The Commonwealth

The Commonwealth arose out of the former British Empire that once included much of Africa and the West Indies, Canada, the Indian sub-continent, Australia and New Zealand. Since 1945, almost all these countries have become independent and together form a loose association called the Commonwealth, with the Crown at its symbolic head.

Only the United Nations is a larger international organisation than the British Commonwealth. The Commonwealth has a membership of 54 states, which together contain 1.7 billion people – 30 per cent of the world's population. Its aims include the development of democracy, good government, and the eradication of poverty, but it has no power over its members other than that of persuasion and only rarely acts together on international issues.

A common language, similarities in culture, and (with some exceptions) mutual recognition of professional qualifications, has greatly assisted the movement of people within the Commonwealth, and had a major effect on migration both to and from Britain.

The United Nations

Britain, like most countries in the world, is a member of the United Nations (UN) – an international organisation, working to prevent war and to maintain international peace and security. Britain is a permanent member of the UN Security Council. The functions of this group include recommending action by the UN in the event of international crises and threats to peace.

Two very important documents produced by the United Nations are the Universal Declaration of Human Rights and the UN Convention on the Rights of the Child. Britain has signed and ratified both of these agreements. Although neither have the force of law, they are important measures by which the behaviour of a state can be judged, and they are increasingly used both in political debate and in legal cases, to reinforce points of law.

REVISION QUESTIONS

Check your understanding of this unit by completing the questions below. Check your answers on page 187

153 When was the Council of Europe established?
ANSWER:

154 What is the purpose of the Council of Europe?
ANSWER:

155 Describe the terms of the first agreement to which European countries committed, which led to the forming of the European Union?
ANSWER:

156 When did Britain join the European Economic Community?
ANSWER:

157 What is the main aim of the European Union today?
ANSWER:

158 What rights do citizens of EU member states have to travel in the EU?
ANSWER:

159 What rights do citizens of EU member states have to work in the EU?
ANSWER:

160 What is the Council of Ministers?
ANSWER:

161 Where is the European Commission based?
ANSWER:

162 What is the role of the European Parliament?
ANSWER:

163 What is an EU Directive?
ANSWER:

164 What is an EU regulation?
ANSWER:

165	What is the total population of all countries that are part of the Commonwealth?
	ANSWER:
166	How many member states are there in the Commonwealth?
	ANSWER:
167	What is the United Nations?
	ANSWER:
168	What is Britain's role within the United Nations?
	ANSWER:

UNIT 6 SUMMARY: BRITAIN IN EUROPE AND THE WORLD

In the Life in the UK Test you could be asked questions about anything included in this unit, but some of the key facts you should remember are:

- Britain was a founding member of the Council of Europe, which was established in 1949. It works to protect human rights and to find solutions to problems facing European society

- The origins of the European Union lie in an agreement made after World War II for various countries to have a single authority controlling all coal and steel production

- Britain joined the European Economic Community in 1973, after twice being vetoed by France

- The main aim of the European Union today is for member states to become a single market

- Citizens of any European Union member country have the right to work in, and travel to, any other member country

- The Council of Ministers is made up of government ministers from European Union member states. It is an influential body that meets periodically to propose new laws and make decisions about how the European Union is run

- The European Commission, based in Brussels, takes care of the day to day running of the European Union

- The European Parliament meets in Strasbourg, France

- Each member country elects Members of the European Parliament (MEPs). The number of MEPs for each country is roughly proportional to national populations

- European Union law overrides national laws of member states. EU laws are mainly regulations and directives, such as those determining how many hours a driver can operate a goods vehicle

- The Commonwealth is an international organisation that works towards the development of democracy, good government and the eradication of poverty

- The Commonwealth arose from the British Empire. The British Empire once included much of Africa, the West Indies, Canada, the Indian sub-continent and Australia and New Zealand

- The Commonwealth has a membership of 54 states, with a total population of 1.7 billion people

- The United Nations is the world's most influential international organisation. It works to prevent war and maintain international peace and security. Britain is a permanent member of the United Nations Security Council

- Two important documents produced by the United Nations are the Universal Declaration of Human Rights and the United Nations Convention on the Rights of the Child

UNIT 7: THE ORDINARY CITIZEN

In this unit you will learn about the political rights enjoyed by every citizen of the United Kingdom. There are many ways that citizens can participate in political life and make a contribution towards the overall good of society. Citizens also have civic duties such as jury service. When studying this unit you should identify which rights guarantee the individual power to have their say, through a vote, on how society should operate.

THE ORDINARY CITIZEN

The right to vote

How does the ordinary citizen connect to government? As we have seen, full democracy came slowly to Britain. Only in 1928 did both men and women aged 21 and over gain the right to vote. The present voting age of 18 was set in 1969.

Both British born and naturalised citizens have full civic rights and duties (such as jury service), including the right to vote in all elections, as long as they are on the electoral register. Permanent residents who are not citizens have all civil and welfare rights except the right to hold a British passport and a general right to vote.

The electoral register

In order to vote in a parliamentary, local, or European election, you must have your name on the register of electors, known as the electoral register. If you are eligible to vote you may register at any time by contacting your local council election registration office. Voter registration forms are also available, in English, Welsh, and a number of other languages, via the Internet from the Electoral Commission, **www.electoralcommission.org.uk**

However the electoral register is also updated annually and an electoral registration form is sent to all households in September or October each year. The form should be completed according to the instructions, and should include everyone eligible to vote who is resident in the household on 15th October.

By law, a local authority has to make the electoral register available for anyone to look at. The register is held at the local electoral registration office (or council office in England and Wales) and some public buildings, such as libraries (however this is not always possible as new regulations require that any viewing of the electoral register is supervised, and libraries do not always have the necessary resources).

You have the right to have your name placed on the electoral register if you are aged 18 or over and a citizen of the United Kingdom, the Commonwealth, or a European Union member state. Citizens of the United Kingdom, the Commonwealth, and the Irish Republic resident in this country may vote in all public elections. Citizens of EU states, resident in the UK, have the right to vote in all but national parliamentary elections.

Participation

The number of people turning out to vote in parliamentary elections in Britain has been falling for several years, especially amongst the young. In the General Election of 2001, less than half of voters below the age of 25 actually voted. The Government and the political parties are looking for ways in which this trend might be reversed.

Standing for office

Citizens of the United Kingdom, the Irish Republic, or the Commonwealth aged 21 or over, may stand for public office. However, there are some exceptions, which include peers, members of the armed forces, civil servants, and those found guilty of certain criminal offices.

To become a local councillor, a candidate must have a local connection with the area, through work, by being on the electoral register, or through renting or owning land or property.

This rule, however, does not apply to MPs, MEPs, or to members of the Scottish Parliament, or the Welsh or Northern Ireland Assemblies. Candidates standing for these bodies must pay a deposit of £500, which is not returned if they receive less than five per cent of the vote. The deposit for candidates standing as a Member of the European Parliament is £5,000. This is to discourage frivolous or hopeless candidates, though many still try their luck.

Contacting elected members

All elected members have a duty to serve and represent the interests of their constituents. Contact details of all your representatives and their parties are available from the local library. Those of Assembly Members, MPs and MEPs are listed in the phone book and Yellow Pages. An MP may be reached either at their constituency office or their office in the House of Commons by letter or phone. The address: House of Commons, Westminster, London SW1A 0AA, tel 0207 219 3000.

Many Assembly Members, MPs and MEPs hold regular local 'surgeries', often on Saturday mornings. These are generally advertised in the local paper, and allow constituents to call in person to raise matters of concern. You can also find out the name of your local MP and get in touch with them by fax through the website, **www.writetothem.com** – this service is free.

REVISION QUESTIONS

Check your understanding of this unit by completing the questions below. Check your answers on page 188

169	What rights and duties do UK citizens have?
	ANSWER:
170	What are the basic requirements for standing for public office?
	ANSWER:
171	How and when do you register to vote?
	ANSWER:
172	How do you contact an elected representative?
	ANSWER:

UNIT 7 SUMMARY: THE ORDINARY CITIZEN

In the Life in the UK Test you could be asked questions about anything included in this unit, but some of the key facts you should remember are:

*   The present voting age of 18 was set in 1969

*   In order to vote your name must be on the electoral register

*   The electoral register is updated annually

*   By law, local authorities are required to make the electoral register available to anyone who wants to look at it

*   Citizens of the United Kingdom, the Irish Republic or the Commonwealth, resident in the United Kingdom, may vote in all public elections

*   In recent times the number of people voting in parliamentary elections has been falling. In the 2001 General Election less than half of voters under 25 cast a vote

- Citizens of the United Kingdom, the Irish Republic or the Commonwealth, aged 21 or over, may stand for public office

- All elected members have a duty to serve and represent the interests of their constituents

- Contact details for all representatives and their parties are held at local libraries

- Many representatives hold local 'surgeries' on Saturday mornings

EXTRA REVISION NOTES

Timeline of British History

This page lists all the key dates in British history that are mentioned in the official study materials.

1534	Church of England established
1605	Gunpowder Plot to blow up the Houses of Parliament
1801	First census held in the UK
mid 1840s	Famine in Ireland
1857	Women granted right to divorce
1882	Women granted right to keep earnings and assets when married
1918	Women over 30 granted right to vote
1918	First World War ends
1922	Northern Ireland Parliament established
1928	Women granted right to vote at the same age as men
1940	Winston Churchill replaces Neville Chamberlain as Prime Minister
1945	End of Second World War
1948	People from Ireland and the West Indies invited to migrate to the UK
1949	Council of Europe created
1952	Coronation of Queen Elizabeth II
1957	Law changed to allow Prime Minister to appoint Life Peers
1969	Voting age changed to 18
1973	Britain joins the European Union
1979	First referendum to establish a Scottish parliament
1990	Margaret Thatcher resigns
1997	Second referendum to establish a Scottish parliament
1998	Good Friday Agreement signed
1999	Creation of the Assembly for Wales and the Scottish Parliament
2001	Last UK census held
2004	Ten new member countries join the EU
2011	Next UK census

British Calendar

This page lists all the key dates of the British calendar that are mentioned in the official study materials.

1 January	New Year
14 February	St Valentine's Day
1 March	St David's Day
17 March	St Patrick's Day
three weeks before Easter	Mothering Sunday
March / April	Easter
1 April	April Fool's Day
23 April	St George's Day
5 November	Guy Fawkes Night
11 November	Remembrance Day
30 November	St Andrew's Day
25 December	Christmas Day
26 December	Boxing Day

WORDS TO KNOW

Below is a list of terms that are used within the official study materials. You will need to know the meaning of some of the terms for the Life in the UK Test. Other terms have been included as background information to help you understand some of the important concepts and facts in the study guide.

10 Downing Street	10 Downing Street is the official residence of the British Prime Minister
A Levels	A Levels are the examinations taken by students in their last year at school, when aged 18
A/S Levels	A/S Levels are the examinations taken by students in their second to last year at school, when aged 17
Abolition	Abolition is the ending of something, such as a practice or tradition
Aging population	An aging population is one where the average age is increasing. This is usually caused by falling birth rates and longer life spans
Anglican Church	The Anglican Church is also known as the Church of England
April Fool's Day	April Fool's Day is the first day in April. People celebrate it by playing jokes on each other
Archbishop of Canterbury	The Archbishop of Canterbury is the head of the Anglican Church
Bank holidays	Bank holidays are public holidays when banks and most businesses must close
Binge drinking	Binge drinking is drinking alcohol to excess. In recent years it has become a major focus of concerns about public disorder and minor crime
Bishop	A Bishop is a senior figure in a Christian church
Bonfire	A large controlled outdoor fire that is lit for ceremony or celebration – especially on Guy Fawkes Night
Boxing Day	Boxing Day is celebrated on 26 December. It was traditionally a day on which people gave gifts to servants, gardeners and other trades people

British Empire	The British Empire included countries and lands formerly colonised by Britain in Africa, the Caribbean, North America, Asia and Australasia
By-election	A by-election is an election held when the representative in a particular constituency either resigns or dies
Cabinet	Cabinet is a committee of about 20 Government Ministers, chaired by the Prime Minister, who meet weekly to decide Government policy
Canvas	To canvas is to actively seek the support of someone, particularly a voter in an election
Census	The Census is a government survey, held every 10 years, that must be completed by all residents
Chancellor of the Exchequer	The Chancellor of the Exchequer is the Minister responsible for economic policy
Civil Service	The Civil Service are independent managers and administrators who carry out Government policy
Cockney	Cockney is the regional accent of people who live in London
Commonwealth	The Commonwealth is an international organisation with a membership of 54 states. It arose out of the remains of the British Empire
Constituency	A constituency is a local area used in elections. People vote for an individual to represent their constituency in the House of Commons
Constitution	A constitution is a set of rules for how a country is governed
Controlled drugs	Controlled drugs are illegal drugs such as heroin, cocaine, ecstasy and cannabis
Convention	A convention is a rule or tradition that is usually unwritten
Coronation	A coronation is the ceremony held when a new Monarch is confirmed

Council of Europe	The Council of Europe is made up of 50 European states. It works to protect human rights and find solutions to European problems
Council of Ministers	The Council of Ministers is made up of Ministers from EU states. It proposes new laws and makes decisions about how the EU is run
Denomination	A denomination is a particular branch of a religion. For example, the Anglican Church is a Christian denomination
Devolved administration	Devolved administration is the principle of central government passing on its powers to regional bodies. This is sometimes called 'Home Rule' as it means decisions about certain government issues can be taken by regional parliaments, such as the Assembly for Wales
Divorce	Divorce is the legal ending of a marriage
Easter eggs	Easter eggs are chocolate eggs given at Easter as gifts
Electoral Register	The electoral register is the list of all people eligible to vote in elections
European Commission	The European Commission is the organisation, based in Brussels, that is responsible for running the activities of the EU
European Economic Community	A former name for the EU
European Union (EU)	An organisation of 25 member states. It allows members to cooperate, particularly on economic matters
Father Christmas	Father Christmas is a mythical figure who distributes presents to children at Christmas
First Past the Post	First Past the Post is the electoral system used in the UK
Football Association (FA)	The Football Association is responsible for running the game of football in England
Foreign Secretary	The Foreign Secretary is the Minister responsible for foreign policy and Britain's relationship with other countries

Free press	Free press means that the media in Britain is not controlled by the Government
Gaelic	Gaelic is the native language of Scotland
GCSE	An abbreviation for the General Certificate of Secondary Education. GCSE examinations are sat by students at the age of 16
General Election	A General Election is held every five years to elect members of the House of Commons
Geordie	Geordie is the regional accent of people who live in Tyneside or Newcastle upon Tyne
Grand National	The Grand National is a horse race held once a year in April
Gunpowder Plot	The Gunpowder Plot of 1605 involved a group of conspirators who plotted to blow up the Houses of Parliament
Guy Fawkes Night	Guy Fawkes Night is held annually to celebrate the thwarting of the Gunpowder Plot
Hansard	Hansard is the official record of all that occurs in parliament
Hard drugs	Hard drugs are the most serious of Controlled Drugs, such as heroin and cocaine
Hereditary Peers	Hereditary Peers used to make up the House of Lords. They inherited their positions from their parents
Home Secretary	The Home Secretary is the Minister responsible for law and order and immigration
House of Commons	The House of Commons is the lower parliamentary assembly
House of Lords	The House of Lords is the upper parliamentary assembly
Houses of Parliament	The Houses of Parliament is used to describe both the House of Commons and the House of Lords
Independent candidate	An independent candidate is a person who tries to be elected to Parliament, but is not part of a political party

Iron Curtain	The Iron Curtain describes the imaginary line that separated western and eastern worlds up until the collapse of the Soviet Union in the late 1980s
Kirk	The Kirk is an alternative name for the Presbyterian Church (Church of Scotland)
Leader of the Opposition	The Leader of the Opposition is the leader of the second largest party in parliament
Legislation	Legislation is the general name given to all laws
Life Peers	Life Peers are appointed by the Prime Minister to sit in the House of Lords
Lord Chancellor	The Lord Chancellor is a government Minister responsible for appointing new judges
Lower House	The Lower House is a Parliament that makes decisions about policy and laws. The Lower House in the United Kingdom is the House of Commons
Member of Parliament (MP)	A Member of Parliament is a representative of the people, elected to sit in the House of Commons
Metropolitan Police	The Metropolitan Police is the police force that serves the people of London
Middle ground	Middle ground is a point of agreement between two opposing views
Minister	A Minister is a senior Government politician with policy and other responsibilities
Monarch	The Monarch describes the Queen or King
Mothering Sunday	Mothering Sunday is a day of celebration where children show appreciation to their mothers
Mugging	The criminal act of stealing in the street by threat or violence
National Assembly for Wales	The National Assembly for Wales is where Welsh representatives meet to determine matters of policy. It is located in Cardiff
National day	A national day, such as St Patrick's Day, celebrates a country and its formation
New Scotland Yard	New Scotland Yard is the headquarters of the Metropolitan Police

Non-departmental Public Bodies	Non-departmental public bodies are agencies set up and funded by the government. They have greater independence than government departments and are generally allowed to operate without direct control by the Ministers or departments that create them
Palace of Westminster	The Palace of Westminster houses the House of Commons and the House of Lords
Parliament	Parliament is where elected national representatives meet to discuss issues and develop laws
Parliament of Scotland	The Parliament of Scotland, situated in Edinburgh, represents the Scottish people
Parliamentary Democracy	A parliamentary democracy describes a country where decisions of government are made by a Parliament of representatives
Party system	A party system is a political system in which representatives and voters organise themselves into groups. These groups usually have shared values and goals
Presbyterian Church	The Presbyterian Church is the Church of Scotland
Pressure Groups	Pressure groups are groups with special interests who seek to influence politicians
Prime Minister	The Prime Minister is the leader of the governing party and chair of the Cabinet
Proportional Representation	Proportional Representation is an electoral system where seats in parliament are allocated to parties according to the proportion of votes received
Protestant	A Protestant is a person that follows the Christian religion. This includes followers of the Anglican Church and the Presbyterian Church
Quango	Quango is another name for a non-departmental public body
Queen's Speech	The Queen's Speech is delivered by the Queen at the beginning of a new session of Parliament setting out Government policies and intentions
Question time	Question time is regularly allocated in the House of Commons when MPs can ask questions of Ministers

Reformation	The Reformation was a movement of the sixteenth century that installed Protestantism as the established religion in Britain
Remembrance Day	Remembrance Day is held each November to remember those who have died at war
Scouse	Scouse is the regional accent of people who live in Liverpool
Shadow Cabinet	The Shadow Cabinet is a group of MPs from the main opposition party in Parliament who are responsible for representing the party on important issues
Speaker	The Speaker in both the House of Commons and House of Lords acts as chair in parliamentary debates
Spin	Spin is the slant put on issues by spokespeople from political parties
St Andrew's Day	The national day of Scotland
St David's Day	The national day of Wales
St George's Day	The national day of England
St Patrick's Day	The national day of Northern Ireland and the Republic of Ireland
St Valentine's Day	St Valentine's Day is held each February to celebrate love and relationships
Stepfamily	A stepfamily is formed when people with children re-marry
Stormont	Stormont is an alternative name for the Northern Ireland Parliament
Supreme Governor	The Supreme Governor is the role performed by the Monarch as head of the Anglican Church
Treasury	The Treasury is the government department responsible for managing all the money that the government receives, holds and spends
United Nations (UN)	The United Nations is a global organisation dedicated to peace, security and human rights

United Nations Security Council	The United Nations Security Council is a committee of 15 members focused on global security. The UK is one of five permanent members
Upper House	An Upper House is a Parliament that reviews decisions about policy and laws. The Upper House in the United Kingdom is the House of Lords
Westminster	Westminster is a general term usually used to describe the government
Whips	Whips are MPs who ensure other MPs from their political party cast their vote in line with party intentions
Wimbledon	Wimbledon is a prestigious tennis tournament held annually in south London

PRACTICE TESTS

Preparation Tips

Before you start

The Life in the UK Test is made up of 24 multiple choice questions. You have 45 minutes to complete the test. This means you have just under two minutes to answer each question. This is plenty of time as long as you concentrate and work steadily. However, don't spend too much time on one question. If you find a question difficult and are unsure of the correct answer then make a note of the question number on your blank paper. Come back to the question once you have completed the rest of the test.

Before you begin the test ask the test supervisor for blank paper. You will not be able to use any other materials during the test, however you can use the supplied paper to make notes during the test, particularly about any questions you find difficult and want to come back to later.

Questions to expect

All questions in the *Life in the UK Test* are multiple choice format. There are four different formats in which a question may be asked:

1. One correct answer – Choose the correct answer to the question from four options

EXAMPLE

When did women first get the right to vote?

A   1840

B   1901

C   1918

D   1945

2. Two correct answers – Choose two correct answers to the question from four options

EXAMPLE

The UK restricted its immigration laws in the 1970s – however which TWO locations did Britain admit refugees from during this time?

A   Ethiopia

B   South East Asia

C   Turkey

D   Uganda

3. True or False – Decide whether a statement is true or false

EXAMPLE

Judges are independent of the Crown. Is this statement true or false?

A   True

B   False

4. Select correct statement – Choose the correct statement from two options

EXAMPLE

Which of these statements is correct?

A   *The House of Lords may reject laws proposed by the House of Commons*

B   *The House of Lords can only delay the passage of new laws*

Working through the answers

When you start your test make sure you read each question carefully. Make sure you understand it.

If you are confident that you know the correct answer then make your selection and move on to the next question.

It is vital that you select an answer for every question even if you are not confident that it is correct. There is a chance that even a guess will be correct! If you do this make sure that you note the question number on your blank paper. It is possible that a question later in the test will help you to answer a question that you have found difficult.

Traps to watch out for

Some questions may be worded so that an option may be a TRUE statement but not be the CORRECT answer to the question being asked.

Be careful if questions and answers use words that are absolute. These words mean that the question or answer applies in all cases (e.g. *always, every*) or not at all (e.g. *never*).

EXAMPLE

Which of these statements is correct?

A   *The Queen must always marry someone who is Protestant*

B   *The Queen must always marry someone who is British*

This question gives the option between two absolute statements. There are no exceptions. In this example, the correct answer is A. The Monarch swears to maintain the Protestant religion in Britain, and must always marry another Protestant.

You also need to be careful of words that *moderate* a question or answer. When words such as *often, rarely, sometimes* and *usually* are used this means that the question or answer is referring to something which is not true in all cases.

EXAMPLE

Where are government statements usually reported as coming from?

A   Buckingham Palace

B   Number Ten

C   Stormont

D   Clarence House

In the above example, it is possible that a government statement might come from other ministers or departments, however in most cases media will report statements as coming from Number Ten. Therefore, option B is the correct answer.

Also watch for negative words in questions or answers – such as *not, never* and *neither.* These words can be easily overlooked and completely change the meaning of the question being asked.

EXAMPLE

Which of the following statements about the Commonwealth is not correct?

A   It has a common language

B   It has a membership of 54 states

C   It has 10% of the world's population

D   The Crown is the symbolic head

In the example above, notice that the question is asking for the statement that is not correct. The Commonwealth does have a common language, comprises 54 member states, and the Crown is the symbolic head. The Commonwealth has 30% of the world's population. Therefore, although option C is a false statement, it is the correct answer for this question.

For some questions one of the answers may read: *all of the above*. In these cases read the other answers carefully to see if it is possible that they are all correct. Even if two of the three answers seem correct, all three alternative answers must be correct for you to choose the *all of the above* option.

For some questions one of the answers may read: *none of the above*. In these cases read the other answers carefully to see if it is possible that they are all incorrect. Even if two of the three answers seem incorrect, all three alternative answers must be wrong for you to choose the *none of the above* option.

PRACTICE TEST 1

1 How long was Britain at war during the Second World War?

A 2 years

B 4 years

C 6 years

D 8 years

2 Why did large numbers of Jewish people come to Britain during 1880–1910?

A To escape famine

B To escape the violence they faced at home

C To invade and seize land

D None of the above

3 When did women first get the right to vote?

A 1840

B 1901

C 1918

D 1945

4 Cigarette consumption in Britain has risen significantly. Is this statement true or false?

A True

B False

5 How often is a census carried out in the United Kingdom?

A Once every five years

B Once every eight years

C Once every ten years

D Whenever the government decides

6   What was the population of the United Kingdom in 2001?

    A 38.3 million

    B 48.1 million

    C 58.8 million

    D 98.3 million

7   According to the 2001 Census, what percentage of the UK population reported that they had a religion?

    A 35%

    B 55%

    C 65%

    D 75%

8   How does the King or Queen select the Archbishop of Canterbury?

    A Based on a public ballot

    B Based on their own judgement as to who would make a good Archbishop

    C Using advice from other bishops

    D Using advice from the Prime Minister who takes a recommendation from a Church appointed committee

9   When is New Year celebrated in the United Kingdom?

    A 25 December

    B 31 December

    C 1 January

    D 1 March

10   What do Easter eggs symbolise?

    A Fertility and progress

    B Good health and proper eating

    C New life and the coming of spring

    D Youth and happiness

11 What does Guy Fawkes Night commemorate?

    A Remembrance of those killed during war

    B The Gunpowder Plot of 1605

    C The invention of fireworks

    D The rebuilding of the Houses of Parliament

12 When is the national day for Scotland?

    A 1 March

    B 17 March

    C 23 April

    D 30 November

13 What type of constitution does the UK have?

    A A legal constitution

    B A written constitution

    C An amended constitution

    D An unwritten constitution

14 What is the name of the ministerial position that is responsible for order and immigration?

    A Chancellor of the Exchequer

    B Chief Whip

    C Home Secretary

    D Lord Chancellor

15 A Prime Minister can be removed from office by their party at any time. Is this statement true or false?

    A True

    B False

16 **Which one of the following parliaments or assemblies does not use proportional representation?**

    A Scottish Parliament

    B Welsh Assembly

    C Northern Ireland Assembly

    D House of Commons

17 **What are the roles of the Whips in parliament?**
Select two correct roles from below

    A Ensure discipline and attendance of MPs at voting time in the House of Commons

    B Ensure the House of Commons is always safe and secure

    C Keep order in the House of Commons during political debates

    D Negotiate with the Speaker over the parliamentary timetable and order of business

18 **What are the two main roles of the House of Lords? Select two options from below**

    A To create and shape new laws

    B To examine laws proposed by the House of Commons in detail and at greater leisure

    C To represent everyone in each member's constituency

    D To suggest amendments or changes to laws proposed by the House of Commons

19 **When are local government elections held?**

    A April every two years

    B June and December each year

    C May each year

    D September each year

20 Which of these statements is correct?

    A The Good Friday Agreement was not endorsed by the Irish and British governments

    B The Northern Ireland Assembly was established shortly after the Good Friday Agreement was signed

21 How many Members of the Scottish Parliament (MSPs) are there?

    A 97

    B 158

    C 129

    D 105

22 Britain was a founding member of the EU. Is this statement true or false?

    A True

    B False

23 Which of these statements is correct?

    A Citizens of the European Union have the right to work in any EU member state

    B Citizens of the European Union must have a valid work permit to work in any EU member state

24 What is the current voting age?

    A 16 years old

    B 18 years old

    C 20 years old

    D 21 years old

PRACTICE TEST 2

1 **Name three countries that Jewish people migrated from (and into the UK) to escape persecution during 1880—1910**

    A France, Germany, Poland

    B Germany, Austria, Italy

    C Poland, Ukraine, Belarus

    D Portugal, Spain, Ukraine

2 **During the 1950s, Britain set up bus driver recruitment centres in which location?**

    A Australia

    B Ireland

    C Canada

    D West Indies

3 **The employment of children in the UK is strictly controlled by law. Is this statement true or false?**

    A True

    B False

4 **Since 1951, the UK population has grown faster than the average growth for countries in the European Union. Is this statement true or false?**

    A True

    B False

5 **What is the population of England?**

    A 23.4 million

    B 38.1 million

    C 49.1 million

    D 58.8 million

6 **The UK birth rate was at an all time high in 2002. Is this statement true or false?**

A True

B False

7 **Which other name can be used to refer to the Church of England?**

A The Anglican Church

B The Catholic Church

C The Methodist Church

D The Presbyterian Church

8 **Where is the Cockney dialect spoken?**

A Cornwall

B Liverpool

C London

D Tyneside

9 **What does Boxing Day celebrate?**

A Appreciation of gifts received on Christmas Day

B Appreciation of work by servants and trades people

C Recycling the packaging used to pack Christmas gifts

D The British Heavyweight Boxing Championship

10 **What is the Grand National?**

A A major UK high street bank

B A popular horse racing event

C A train connecting London and Cardiff

D The name of the national lottery

11 What does Remembrance Day commemorate?

   A The appreciation of single mothers

   B The celebration of community

   C The crucifixion of Jesus Christ

   D The memory of those who died during war

12 What does the British abbreviation FA stand for?

   A A Federal Agent

   B The Football Association

   C The Fourth Amendment

   D The Fine Arts

13 How is it decided which party forms the Government?

   A The members of the House of Lords vote for their preferred party

   B The party with the most candidates forms the Government

   C The party with the most MPs elected into the House of Commons forms the Government

   D The party with the most votes forms the Government

14 What happens to policy & law decisions once they have been agreed by Cabinet?

   A They are published in local newspapers for public debate

   B They are signed by the Prime Minister making them law

   C They are submitted to Parliament for approval

   D They are submitted to the King or Queen for royal assent

15 How often does the Cabinet normally meet?

   A Daily

   B Weekly

   C Bi-weekly

   D Monthly

16 Members of the public are not able to visit the Houses of Parliament. Is this statement true or false?

    A True

    B False

17 Who is the current heir to the throne?

    A The Duke of Edinburgh

    B The Duke of York

    C Prince William

    D The Prince of Wales

18 It is possible for a candidate to win a constituency even if they don't win more than half of the votes cast. Is this statement true or false?

    A False

    B True

19 Where do local authorities get most of their funding from?

    A Central government taxation

    B Lottery grants

    C Issuing parking tickets

    D Local council tax

20 What can the Scottish Parliament do that the Welsh Assembly can not? Select two options from below

    A Appoint Members of the Scottish Parliament to the House of Lords

    B Debate laws governing defence, foreign affairs and social security

    C Make changes in the lower base rate of income tax

    D Pass legislation on anything not specifically reserved for Westminster

21 Non-departmental public bodies are a direct part of the civil service. Is this statement true or false?

    A True

    B False

22 **The British Commonwealth is a larger international organisation than the United Nations. Is this statement true or false?**

    A True

    B False

23 **What is the role of the Council of Ministers?**

    A Debate proposals, decisions and expenditure of the European Commission

    B Judge and give verdicts on European court cases that have been appealed

    C Ensure EU regulations and directives are being followed by other member states

    D Propose new laws and decisions regarding the EU

24 **From the list below, which is not a right or duty of UK citizens?**

    A Right to vote in all elections

    B Duty to perform jury service

    C Duty to perform military service

    D Right to welfare benefits

PRACTICE TEST 3

1 **Which countries were invited to provide immigrant workers to help British reconstruction after the Second World War?**

    A Canada and France

    B Germany and Holland

    C Ireland and the West Indies

    D Poland and Ukraine

2 **What percentage of children live with both birth parents?**

    A 45%

    B 50%

    C 65%

    D 80%

3 **When did married women gain the right to retain ownership of their own money and property?**

    A 1752

    B 1792

    C 1810

    D 1882

4 **There are more men in study at university than women. Is this statement true or false?**

    A True

    B False

5 **When was the first census carried out in the United Kingdom?**

    A 1785

    B 1801

    C 1851

    D 1912

6 What is the population of Northern Ireland?

    A 0.9 million

    B 1.7 million

    C 2.5 million

    D 3.1 million

7 What year did the Church of England come in to existence?

    A 1444

    B 1534

    C 1644

    D 1754

8 What is the distance of the widest part across England and Wales?

    A Approximately 500 kilometres

    B Approximately 1,000 kilometres

    C Approximately 2,000 kilometres

    D Approximately 10,000 kilometres

9 What tradition is observed in the period before Remembrance Day?

    A People dress in black

    B People eat Remembrance Cakes

    C People give flowers to community elders

    D People wear artificial poppies in buttonholes

10 What does Easter commemorate?

    A The appointment of a new Archbishop

    B The birth of Jesus Christ

    C The creation of the Church of England

    D The resurrection of Jesus Christ

11 According to tradition, when are Christmas presents opened?

    A On Boxing Day

    B On Christmas Day

    C On Christmas Eve

    D On New Year's Eve

12 When is the national day for England?

    A 1 March

    B 17 March

    C 23 April

    D 30 November

13 What is the role of the Cabinet?

    A To decide general policies for government

    B To examine laws proposed by the House of Commons

    C To investigate serious complaints against the police

    D To provide royal assent for new laws

14 When are by-elections held?

    A Every six months

    B Every two years

    C Every three years

    D Only when an MP resigns or dies while in office

15 How many politicians are there in the Cabinet?

    A About 10

    B About 20

    C About 30

    D About 40

16 **Which of the following parliaments or assemblies use proportional representation?**

    A European Parliament

    B Northern Ireland Assembly

    C Scottish Parliament

    D All of the above

17 **In which year did Queen Elizabeth II start her reign?**

    A 1945

    B 1952

    C 1963

    D 1972

18 **Where is the House of Commons?**

    A In Buckingham Palace

    B In the Palace of Westminster

    C In Windsor Castle

    D In Clarence House

19 **What are the two key features of the civil service? Select two options from below**

    A Business knowledge

    B Neutrality

    C Party loyalty

    D Professionalism

20 **When did the government start a programme of devolved administration for Wales and Scotland?**

    A 1979

    B 1982

    C 1997

    D 2001

21 When is Remembrance Day?

    A 1 May

    B 31 August

    C 21 October

    D 11 November

22 Almost all of the countries that are members of the Commonwealth are now independent of Britain. Is this statement true or false?

    A True

    B False

23 What is the role of the European Parliament?

    A Propose new laws and make decisions regarding the EU

    B Ensure EU regulations and directives are being followed by member states

    C Judge and give verdicts on European court cases that have been appealed

    D To scrutinise and debate the proposals, decisions and expenditure of the European Commission

24 What is the minimum age for standing for public office?

    A 18 years

    B 21 years

    C 25 years

    D 30 years

PRACTICE TEST 4

1   What work did migrant Irish labourers do in the UK during the Irish famine?

   A   Construct canals and railways

   B   Drive local buses

   C   Teach in schools

   D   Work in textile mills

2   What proportion of women with children (of school age) also work?

   A   One quarter

   B   Half

   C   Two thirds

   D   Three quarters

3   Very few people believe that women in Britain should stay at home and not go out to paid work. Is this statement true or false?

   A   True

   B   False

4   At what ages do school children take compulsory tests?

   A   5, 10 and 15

   B   6, 10 and 14

   C   7, 11 and 14

   D   8, 12 and 15

5   In which year will the next UK census be carried out?

   A   2008

   B   2011

   C   2015

   D   2020

6   How much has the UK population grown by (in percentage terms) since 1951?

    A   5%

    B   17%

    C   23%

    D   34%

7   Who ceremonially appoints a new Archbishop of Canterbury?

    A   The exiting Archbishop of Canterbury

    B   The Home Secretary

    C   The King or Queen

    D   The Prime Minister

8   Welsh is no longer taught in schools in Wales. Is this statement true or false?

    A   True

    B   False

9   Where is it believed that Father Christmas folklore originated?

    A   From Dutch, German and Swedish settlers emigrating to America

    B   From early Catholic beliefs

    C   From Russian tsars wanting to encourage gift giving

    D   From Christmas advertising campaigns for a major soft drink company

10   In which year were the Assembly for Wales and the Scottish Parliament created?

    A   1969

    B   1972

    C   1982

    D   1999

11 **What is the name of the patron saint of Scotland?**

    A St Andrew

    B St David

    C St George

    D St Patrick

12 **When is Christmas celebrated?**

    A 25 November

    B 24 December

    C 25 December

    D 1 January

13 **What is the name of the ministerial position that is responsible for the economy?**

    A Chancellor of the Exchequer

    B Chief Whip

    C Home Secretary

    D Lord Chancellor

14 **Newspapers can not publish political opinions or run campaigns to influence government. Is this statement true or false?**

    A True

    B False

15 **How often are general elections held in the UK?**

    A At least once every two years

    B At least once every three years

    C At least once every five years

    D At least once every six years

16 **Judges are independent of the Crown. Is this statement true or false?**

    A True

    B False

17 **Select the two correct ceremonial duties that the King or Queen performs from the options below**

    A Chairing proceedings in the House of Lords

    B Debating political opinions with the Prime Minister

    C Opening and closing of parliament

    D Reading the "Queen's (or King's) Speech"

18 **The Scottish Parliament has powers to vary national income tax. Is this statement true or false?**

    A True

    B False

19 **Who from the list below is not responsible for controlling the administration of the police?**

    A Chief of Police

    B Elected local councillors

    C Home Secretary

    D Magistrates

20 **Where is the National Assembly for Wales situated?**

    A Cardiff

    B Edinburgh

    C Stormont

    D Swansea

21 **Which of these statements is correct?**

    A The House of Lords may reject laws proposed by the House of Commons

    B The House of Lords can only delay the passage of new laws

22 Which of the following statements about the Commonwealth is not correct?

    A It has a common language

    B It has a membership of 54 states

    C It has 10% of the world's population

    D The Crown is the symbolic head

23 Which of these statements is correct?

    A EU Directives automatically have force in all EU member states

    B EU Directives must be introduced and observed within EU member states within a specific time frame

24 To become a local councillor, a candidate must have a local connection with the area. Is this statement true or false?

    A True

    B False

PRACTICE TEST 5

1 **During 1948, what were immigrants from Ireland and the West Indies invited into the UK to do?**

    A Work in textile mills

    B Aid the reconstruction effort after the Second World War

    C Drive buses and taxis in local towns and villages

    D Help build canals and railways

2 **What is the percentage difference in pay between male and female hourly pay rates?**

    A Women receive 5% lower pay than men

    B Women receive 10% lower pay than men

    C Women receive 20% lower pay than men

    D No difference - women are paid the same as men

3 **When do young people take GCSE examinations?**

    A 15 years old

    B 16 years old

    C 17 years old

    D 18 years old

4 **What percentage of the workforce are women?**

    A 40%

    B 45%

    C 51%

    D 65%

5 How many years must have passed before an individual's census form is viewable by the public?

    A 10 years

    B 50 years

    C 100 years

    D An individual's census form is confidential and never viewable by the public

6 What is the largest ethnic minority in Britain?

    A Bangladeshi descent

    B Black Caribbean descent

    C Indian descent

    D Pakistani descent

7 What are the two most widespread Christian denominations in Wales? Select two options from below

    A Baptist

    B Catholic

    C Methodist

    D Presbyterian

8 Where is the Welsh language widely spoken?

    A Highlands and Islands of Scotland

    B Ireland

    C Southern England

    D Wales

9 When did the First World War end?

    A 28 February 1914

    B 11 November 1918

    C 21 November 1925

    D 8 May 1945

10 **When is St Valentine's Day?**

    A 1 February

    B 14 February

    C 1 April

    D 14 April

11 **Where is the popular UK tennis tournament played in South London?**

    A Putney

    B Richmond

    C Twickenham

    D Wimbledon

12 **When is the national day for Wales?**

    A 1 March

    B 17 March

    C 23 April

    D 30 November

13 **What is the name of the ministerial position that is responsible for foreign affairs?**

    A Chancellor of the Exchequer

    B Foreign Secretary

    C Home Secretary

    D Lord Chancellor

14 **What is the name of the official record of proceedings in Parliament?**

    A Hansard

    B Parliament News

    C The Recorder

    D Westminster Hour

15 **Which politicians are members of the Shadow Cabinet?**

   A   The remaining MPs in Government who are not in the Cabinet

   B   Peers from the House of Lords

   C   Civil servants working for the government

   D   Senior members of the main opposition party

16 **The Government has the power to instruct the police to arrest or proceed against an individual. Is this statement true or false?**

   A   True

   B   False

17 **Who is the Head of State of the United Kingdom?**

   A   The Home Secretary

   B   The King or Queen

   C   The Prime Minister

   D   The Speaker of the House of Commons

18 **Which of the following is not a service provided by local authorities?**

   A   Education

   B   Refuse collection

   C   Fire service

   D   None – they are all services provided by local authorities

19 **Which of these statements is correct?**

   A   The headquarters of the Metropolitan Police is based at New Scotland Yard

   B   The Metropolitan Police has headquarters based at the Palace of Westminster

20 How many Assembly Members are there in the National Assembly for Wales?

    A About 30 members

    B About 40 members

    C About 50 members

    D About 60 members

21 The Council of Ministers has no power to propose new laws. Is this statement true or false?

    A True

    B False

22 What is the purpose of the United Nations?

    A To prevent war and maintain peace and security

    B To create a single market for all world nations

    C To create global laws to regulate foreign affairs

    D To debate global third world development and funding proposals

23 Which two statements describe features of an EU regulation? Select two options from below

    A EU Regulations must be adopted and implemented by each EU member state by a set time

    B EU Regulations automatically have force in all EU member states

    C EU Regulations can not override national legislation

    D EU Regulations override national legislation

24 How do you register to vote?

    A Complete an electoral registration form

    B Do nothing – all eligible citizens are automatically registered

    C Bring your passport to any polling booth on election day

    D Contact your local MP's office

PRACTICE TEST 6

1 The UK restricted its immigration laws in the 1970s – however which two locations did Britain admit refugees from during this time?

    A Ethiopia

    B South East Asia

    C Turkey

    D Uganda

2 How often do most children in the UK receive their pocket money?

    A Every day

    B Every month

    C Every week

    D Only on their birthday

3 When do young people take A/S and A level examinations?

    A 14 and 15 years old

    B 15 and 16 years old

    C 16 and 17 years old

    D 17 and 18 years old

4 Why was a census not carried out in the United Kingdom in 1941?

    A Because Britain was at war

    B Because it was abolished by the government

    C Because it was boycotted by the public

    D No census was planned for that year

5 What is the population of Scotland?

    A 1.3 million

    B 3.2 million

    C 5.1 million

    D 7.8 million

6 What percentage of the UK population is made up of ethnic minorities?

    A About 2%

    B About 8%

    C About 15%

    D About 25%

7 What is the estimated percentage of population that regularly attend church services in England?

    A Between 4% and 7%

    B Between 8% and 11%

    C Between 12% and 15%

    D Between 16% and 20%

8 Where is the Gaelic language spoken?

    A Highlands and Islands of Scotland

    B Cornwall

    C Southern England

    D Wales

9 What is traditionally eaten on Christmas Day?

    A Beer battered cod and chips

    B Poached salmon and rice pudding

    C Roast pork and trifle

    D Roast turkey and Christmas Pudding

10 According to tradition if you were the first visitor of the new year to a Scottish home, what might you be expected to bring?

    A A bag of ice and whisky

    B A block of butter and whisky

    C Coal, bread and whisky

    D Milk, tartan cloth and whisky

11 What is the name of the patron saint of England?

    A St Andrew

    B St David

    C St George

    D St Patrick

12 How many bank holidays are there each year in the United Kingdom?

    A Two

    B Four

    C Nine

    D Ten

13 Where is the Prime Minister's official residence?

    A 10 Downing Street

    B 12 Downing Street

    C Buckingham Palace

    D Westminster Palace

14 What is the abbreviation MP short for?

    A Master of Parliament

    B Member of Parliament

    C Member of Party

    D Minister of Parliament

15 **The monarch can reject laws and decisions made by government and the Cabinet. Is this statement true or false?**

    A True

    B False

16 **Political party membership in Britain has been declining rapidly in the last few years. Is this statement true or false?**

    A True

    B False

17 **What other regional language, in addition to English, is also spoken in Scotland?**

    A French

    B Welsh

    C Gaelic

    D Scottish

18 **How are new judges selected?**

    A All lawyers with over twenty years experience may enter a lottery ballot

    B By a special parliamentary committee

    C From nominations put forward by existing judges

    D The King or Queen takes advice from the Prime Minister

19 **What is the name of the largest police force in the United Kingdom?**

    A Humberside

    B Merseyside

    C The Bill

    D The Metropolitan Police

20 **When was the first referendum for a Scottish Parliament?**

    A 1962

    B 1979

    C 1987

    D 1997

21 **Where is the European Commission based?**

    A Paris

    B Geneva

    C Strasbourg

    D Brussels

22 **What is the purpose of the Council of Europe?**

    A To create a single market for participating members of the council

    B To debate proposals, decisions and expenditure of the European Commission

    C To protect human rights and seek solutions to problems facing European society

    D To create new European regulations and directives

23 **How many member states are there in the Commonwealth?**

    A 25 member states

    B 39 member states

    C 54 member states

    D 75 member states

24 **How can you meet with your local MP?**

    A By attending a local surgery

    B By inviting them to dinner

    C By visiting the House of Commons

    D By visiting your local town hall

PRACTICE TEST 7

1 During the 1980s, the seven largest immigrant groups to the UK were from the United States, Australia, South Africa, New Zealand, Hong Kong, Singapore and Malaysia. Is this statement true or false?

    A True

    B False

2 How many young people (up to the age of 19) are there in the UK?

    A 5 million

    B 10 million

    C 15 million

    D 20 million

3 What is the minimum age for buying alcohol?

    A 14 years old

    B 16 years old

    C 18 years old

    D 21 years old

4 Over the last 20 years, there has been a decline in population in the north east and north west of England. Is this statement true or false?

    A True

    B False

5 What is the population of Wales?

    A 1.2 million

    B 2.9 million

    C 3.4 million

    D 5.3 million

6 **According to the Church of England, heirs to the throne are not allowed to marry whom?**

    A Anyone who is not of royal blood

    B Anyone who is not Protestant

    C Anyone who is under the age of 25

    D Anyone who was born outside the UK

7 **What must a monarch swear to do as part of their coronation?**

    A To advise the Prime Minister on state affairs

    B To appoint their heir to the throne

    C To maintain the protestant religion in the United Kingdom

    D To reign as monarch for at least 20 years

8 **What is the distance from the north coast of Scotland to the south coast of England?**

    A Approximately 500 kilometres

    B Approximately 1,000 kilometres

    C Approximately 2,000 kilometres

    D Approximately 10,000 kilometres

9 **What is mistletoe traditionally used for during Christmas?**

    A Burned in the fireplace as an aromatic fuel

    B Given to friends and relatives as a symbol of Christmas generosity

    C Hung above doorways under which couples are expected to kiss

    D Used as a spice to make Christmas Pudding

10 **When is Mothering Sunday?**

    A One week before Easter

    B Two weeks before Easter

    C Three weeks before Easter

    D Four weeks before Easter

11 What is the name of the patron saint of Northern Ireland?

    A St Andrew

    B St David

    C St George

    D St Patrick

12 What does Christmas day celebrate?

    A The birth of Jesus Christ

    B The death of Jesus Christ

    C The miracles of Jesus Christ

    D The resurrection of Jesus Christ

13 What happens during Question Time?

    A Government Ministers present new policies for debate

    B Members of Parliament may ask questions of Government Ministers

    C Members of Parliament take questions from the press

    D Members of the public can ask questions of their local MP

14 Which of the following statements is not true about the constitutional role of the monarch? Select two options from below

    A They must always follow the Prime Minister's advice

    B They may express their political opinions in public

    C They should criticise government policy if they do not believe it serves the public interest

    D They are responsible for opening and closing parliament

15 In the past, what were the only two ways that members could be appointed to the House of Lords? Select two answers from below

    A By being hereditary aristocrats

    B By being rewarded with peerage for their public service

    C By being voted into the House of Lords by public election

    D By serving at least twenty years as an MP in the House of Commons

16 **The House of Lords can overrule the decisions of the House of Commons. Is this statement true or false?**

    A True

    B False

17 **How many constituencies are there throughout the United Kingdom?**

    A 350

    B 645

    C 750

    D 1,105

18 **What is a Civil Servant?**

    A Any person who has a job carrying out government policy

    B Any person who is a member of a political party

    C Any person who is a Member of Parliament

    D Any person who works for a member of the House of Lords

19 **Who appoints new judges?**

    A Chief Justice

    B Home Secretary

    C King or Queen

    D Lord Chancellor

20 **How many members are there in the Northern Ireland Assembly?**

    A 64 members

    B 82 members

    C 108 members

    D 125 members

21 The Council of Europe has no power to make laws. Is this statement true or false?

A True

B False

22 When was the Council of Europe established?

A 1964

B 1982

C 1901

D 1949

23 What is Britain's role within the United Nations?

A Member of the UN Security Council

B Provides a neutral location for hosting UN meetings in Scotland

C Selects the UN Secretary General from members of the Security Council

D All of the above

24 Which of the following statements about the electoral register is not correct?

A British citizens have the right to have their name placed on the electoral register

B Local authorities must make the electoral register available for anyone to view

C The register is held at local electoral registration offices

D You must be at least 21 years old to have your name on the register

PRACTICE TEST 8

1   Why did Protestant Huguenots from France come to Britain?

    A To escape famine

    B To escape religious persecution

    C To invade and seize land

    D To seek refuge from war

2   What proportion of young people enrol to go on to higher education after school?

    A One in two

    B One in three

    C One in four

    D All young people move on to higher education

3   How many children (under 18) are estimated to be working in the United Kingdom at any time?

    A One million

    B Two million

    C Five million

    D Eight million

4   What percentage of UK's ethnic minorities live in the London area?

    A 14%

    B 30%

    C 45%

    D 60%

5   Britain has an aging population and has a record number of people aged 85 and over. Is this statement true or false?

    A True

    B False

6 **The Queen must not marry anyone who is not Protestant. Is this statement true or false?**

    A True

    B False

7 **What percentage of the British population are Roman Catholic?**

    A 10%

    B 20%

    C 30%

    D 40%

8 **Where is the Scouse dialect spoken?**

    A Cornwall

    B Liverpool

    C London

    D Tyneside

9 **What traditionally happens on St Valentine's Day?**

    A Couples fast from eating

    B Couples visit the elderly together

    C Couples play tricks on each other

    D Couples send cards to each other

10 **What traditionally happens on Mothering Sunday?**

    A Mothers make special meals for their family

    B People hold fireworks displays

    C People celebrate the mother of Jesus Christ

    D People give gifts to their mothers

11 What is the name of the patron saint of Wales?

    A St Andrew

    B St David

    C St George

    D St Patrick

12 Where are government statements usually reported as coming from?

    A Buckingham Palace

    B Number Ten

    C Stormont

    D Clarence House

13 Which of the following statements is correct about political reporting in the UK? Select two options from below

    A All reporting on radio and television must be balanced

    B Politicians must be able to read interview questions beforehand

    C Newspapers usually have their own angle in reporting political events

    D It is illegal for newspapers to run campaigns to influence government policy

14 During a general election, the main parties are given free time on radio and television to make short party political broadcasts. Is this statement true or false?

    A True

    B False

15 Which of these statements is correct?

    A It is illegal to possess cannabis anywhere

    B It is legal to possess cannabis in the privacy of your own home

16 How is the Speaker of the House of Commons chosen?

    A Appointed by the King or Queen

    B Chosen by the Prime Minister

    C Elected by fellow MPs

    D Elected by the public

17 What is the name of the system that governs how MPs are elected into the House of Commons?

    A Aggregated vote system

    B Electoral college system

    C First past the post system

    D Proportional representation system

18 All candidates standing for office in local government must be members of a political party. Is this statement true or false?

    A True

    B False

19 Can a judge challenge the legality of a law?

    A Yes, but only if they do not believe the law is fair

    B Yes, but they must obtain permission from the Lord Chancellor

    C Yes, but they must seek the Prime Minister's approval first

    D No, but they can declare a law incompatible with human rights

20 When was the Good Friday Agreement signed?

    A 1945

    B 1956

    C 1973

    D 1998

21 How often are elections held for Members of the European Parliament?

    A Every two years

    B Every three years

    C Every four years

    D Every five years

22 What were the terms of the first agreement that European countries committed to, which led to the forming of the European Union?

    A To allow free and unrestricted travel for citizens of all member states

    B To agree to adopt a single currency

    C To form a single European parliament that would shape common European legislation

    D To put all their coal and steel production under the control of a single authority

23 Which country does not have its own parliament or national assembly?

    A England

    B Northern Ireland

    C Scotland

    D Wales

24 When was the current voting age set?

    A 1945

    B 1956

    C 1969

    D 1982

PRACTICE TEST 9

1   **During the 1950s, textile and engineering firms
    from the UK sent recruitment agents to which two
    countries? Select two countries from below**

   A   India

   B   Pakistan

   C   Poland

   D   South Africa

2   **When did women get voting rights at the same age as men?**

   A   1840

   B   1918

   C   1928

   D   1945

3   **In the 2001 general election, what proportion of
    first time voters actually cast their vote?**

   A   One in two

   B   One in three

   C   One in five

   D   One in eight

4   **What overall proportion of Britain's African Caribbean, Pakistani,
    Indian and Bangladeshi communities were born in Britain?**

   A   About one quarter

   B   About one third

   C   About half

   D   About three quarters

5   What percentage of London's population is made up of ethnic minorities?

    A 9% of London's population

    B 15% of London's population

    C 29% of London's population

    D 45% of London's population

6   According to the 2001 Census, what percentage of people stated their religion as Muslim?

    A 1%

    B 3%

    C 15%

    D 21%

7   What is the Church of Scotland also known as?

    A The Kirk

    B The Murray

    C The Stormont

    D The Westminster

8   Where is the Geordie dialect spoken?

    A Cornwall

    B Liverpool

    C London

    D Tyneside

9   When is Easter celebrated?

    A In December or January each year

    B In June or July each year

    C In March or April each year

    D In May or June each year

10   When is April Fool's Day?

    A   1 February

    B   1 March

    C   1 April

    D   1 May

11   Which of the UK national days is celebrated with a public holiday?

    A   St Andrew's Day in Scotland

    B   St David's Day in Wales

    C   St George's Day in England

    D   St Patrick's Day in Northern Ireland

12   What is the role of the Speaker in the House of Commons?

    A   To chair proceedings in the House of Commons

    B   To ensure discipline and attendance of MPs at voting time in the House of Commons

    C   To promote Members from the House of Commons to the House of Lords

    D   To sign new laws agreed in the House of Commons

13   What is the role of the Prime Minister? Select two options from below

    A   Appoints ministers of state and other public positions

    B   Leader of the party in power

    C   Make new laws effective by signing legislation

    D   Perform the duties of Head of State

14   Where does the monarch deliver their speech from at the start of a new parliamentary session?

    A   From a throne in Buckingham Palace

    B   From a throne in the House of Lords

    C   From a throne in the House of Commons

    D   From a throne in Windsor Castle

15 **Which of the following statements about non-departmental public bodies is not correct?**

    A Parliament can abolish or change their powers and roles

    B They may propose new laws to the House of Commons

    C They are semi-independent agencies set up by the government

    D They are sometimes called quangos

16 **What famous phrase describes the level of expression that the monarch is restricted to when discussing government matters?**

    A Advise, warn and encourage

    B Advocate, promote and support

    C Direct, track and monitor

    D Discuss, debate and review

17 **In what year did the Prime Minister gain powers to be able to appoint members of the House of Lords?**

    A 1957

    B 1968

    C 1973

    D 1980

18 **Which of the following statements is not true about British politics?**

    A Political party membership in Britain has been declining over the last few years

    B Main political parties have membership branches in every constituency

    C There are no independent MPs in parliament

    D Public opinion polls are very important to the leadership of political parties

19 **Which of the following would not be considered part of a lobby group?**

    A Commercial organisations

    B Industrial organisations

    C Ordinary citizens

    D Professional organisations

20 When was the Northern Ireland Parliament established?

    A 1922

    B 1938

    C 1945

    D 1956

21 Which of the following statements about the European Parliament is not correct?

    A It debates and scrutinises decisions of the European Commission

    B It decides EU policy

    C It has the power to refuse to agree EU expenditure

    D It is based in Strasbourg

22 When did Britain join the European Economic Community?

    A 1935

    B 1959

    C 1973

    D 1992

23 What is the population of all countries that are part of the Commonwealth?

    A 500 million people

    B 900 million people

    C 1.7 billion people

    D 3.5 billion people

24 Citizens from which of the following countries are not eligible to stand for office in the UK?

    A Citizens from Commonwealth countries

    B European citizens

    C Irish Republic citizens

    D United Kingdom citizens

PRACTICE TEST 10

1   Why did Irish migrants come to Britain during the mid 1840s?

  A   To escape famine

  B   To escape religious persecution

  C   To invade and seize land

  D   To seek refuge from war

2   What year did women in the UK gain the right to divorce their husband?

  A   1810

  B   1857

  C   1901

  D   1945

3   What is the minimum age for buying tobacco?

  A   14 years old

  B   16 years old

  C   18 years old

  D   21 years old

4   What percentage of the United Kingdom's population is made up of ethnic minorities?

  A   1.3%

  B   7.9%

  C   10.8%

  D   22.3%

5   What percentage of the UK's population live in England?

  A   53%

  B   68%

  C   75%

  D   83%

6 **According to the 2001 Census, what proportion of people stated their religion as Christian?**

    A Two people out of ten

    B Five people out of ten

    C Seven people out of ten

    D Nine people out of ten

7 **What is the title of the King or Queen within the Church of England?**

    A Archbishop of Canterbury

    B Governor General

    C Head Priest

    D Supreme Governor

8 **When is Guy Fawkes Night?**

    A The evening of 15 October

    B The evening of 25 September

    C The evening of 30 May

    D The evening of 5 November

9 **If you were visiting a Welsh home at New Year, what tradition might be observed?**

    A A new door matt is placed at the front door to welcome visitors into the new year

    B The back door is opened to release the old year, then shut and locked, and then the front door opened to let in the new year

    C All of the windows of the house are opened for an hour to release the old year

    D All of the above

10 **What traditionally happens on April Fool's Day?**

    A It is a public holiday until noon

    B People play jokes on each other

    C People enjoy public firework displays

    D None of the above

11 **When is the national day for Northern Ireland?**

A 1 March

B 17 March

C 23 April

D 30 November

12 **What is the second largest party in the House of Commons called by convention?**

A Her Majesty's Loyal Opposition

B Shadow Cabinet

C The Conservation Party

D The Labour Party

13 **What did the Prime Minister used to be called in Latin?**

A Primus dominis

B Primus inter pares

C Primus obter dictum

D Primus ad mortem

14 **How are Whips appointed?**

A By their party leaders

B By the King or Queen

C By the Prime Minister

D By vote amongst their peers

15 **Who of the following are automatically members of the House of Lords? Choose two answers from below**

A Mayors from local government

B Most senior judges

C Senior Bishops of the Church of England

D MPs who are also members of the Cabinet

16 What must a candidate achieve in order to win their constituency?

    A Be a member of the party that wins government office

    B Win at least 25% of the votes within their constituency

    C Win at least 15,000 votes

    D Win the most votes out of all candidates in their constituency

17 What is a Life Peer?

    A A hereditary aristocrat or peer of the realm

    B A member of the House of Lords who has been appointed by the Prime Minister

    C Any person who has inherited a peerage from their family

    D Any person who has served as a MP for more than twenty years

18 Who is responsible for investigating serious complaints against the police?

    A The Lord Chancellor

    B The Home Secretary

    C The Chief of Police

    D An independent authority

19 When was the civil service reformed to prevent corruption and favouritism?

    A Early 15th century

    B Early 17th century

    C Early 18th century

    D Early 19th century

20 When was the second referendum for a Scottish Parliament?

    A 1962

    B 1979

    C 1987

    D 1997

21 How many members are there in the Council of Europe?

   A   10 member states

   B   20 member states

   C   50 member states

   D   60 member states

22 What is the main aim behind the European Union today?

   A   For member states to observe a single set of laws

   B   For member states to improve efficiency

   C   For member states to protect human rights in Europe

   D   For member states to become a single market

23 Which of the following is not a requirement for MPs, MEPs or MSPs wishing to stand for office?

   A   A local connection within the area in which they wish to take office

   B   Citizenship of the United Kingdom, the Irish Republic or the Commonwealth

   C   Be over the age of 21 years old

   D   Be willing and able to pay a deposit to support their campaign

24 What must a candidate have in order to become a local councillor?

   A   A connection with the area in which they wish to take office

   B   A deposit of £500

   C   A recommendation from their local MP

   D   Membership of a political party

शब्दों को जानें

नीचे दिए गए शब्द सरकारी अध्ययन सामग्री में प्रयुक्त किए गए हैं। लाईफ़ इन UK टेस्ट में कुछ शब्दों का अर्थ जानने की आपको आवश्यकता पड़ेगी। अन्य शब्द पृष्ठभूमि सूचना के रूप में सम्मिलित किए गए हैं जो आपको कुछ महत्वपूर्ण अवधारणाओं तथा तथ्यों को अध्ययन मार्गदर्शन में समझाने में सहायता करेंगे।

10 Downing Street	ब्रिटिश प्रधानमंत्री का सरकारी आवास
A Levels	ए लेवल (A Levels) वे परीक्षाएँ हैं जो विद्यार्थियों को अपने स्कूल के अंतिम वर्ष में देनी होती हैं जब उनकी उम्र 18 साल होती है
A/S Levels	ए / एस लेवल (A/S Levels) वे परीक्षाएँ हैं, जो विद्यार्थियों को अपने स्कूल के दूसरे वर्ष में देनी होती हैं जब उनकी उम्र 17 साल होती है
Abolition	उन्मूलन (Abolition) किसी चीज़ का समाप्त होना जैसे व्यवहार या परंपरा का
Aging population	प्रौढ़ जनसंख्या (Aging population) वह है जहाँ औसत आयु बढ़ रही है। यह सामान्य तौर पर जन्म दर घटने तथा जीवन अवधि लंबी होने से होता है
Anglican Church	एंग्लिकन (Anglican) चर्च को इंग्लैंड के गिरजाघर (Church of England) के तौर पर भी जाना जाता है
April Fool's Day	अप्रैल फूल्स दिवस (April Fool's Day) अप्रैल माह का पहला दिवस है। इसे लोग एक दूसरे से मज़ाक कर मनाते हैं
Archbishop of Canterbury	केन्टरबरी के मुख्य पादरी (Archbishop of Canterbury) एंग्लिकन चर्च के प्रमुख हैं
Bank holidays	बैंक अवकाश (Bank holidays) वे सार्वजनिक अवकाश हैं जब बैंक तथा अधिकांश व्यवसाय बंद होता है
Binge drinking	बिंज ड्रिंकिंग (Binge drinking) का अर्थ है बहुत अधिक शराब (अल्कोहोल) पीना। कुछ वर्षों से ये आम गड़बड़ी व लघु अपराधों के मामले में चिंता का मुख्य कारण बन गया है
Bishop	पादरी (Bishop) ईसाई गिरजे का एक वरिष्ठ व्यक्ति होता है
Bonfire	एक बड़ी नियंत्रित आग जिसे किसी समारोह या उत्सव मनाने के लिए जलाया जाता है – विशेष रूप से गाई फ़ॉक्स नाईट को

Boxing Day	बॉक्सिंग दिवस (Boxing Day) 26 दिसंबर को मनाया जाता है। ये पारंपरिक रूप से एक दिन होता है जहाँ लोग उनके नौकरों, मालियों तथा अन्य धंधे के लोगों को उपहार देते हैं
British Empire	ब्रिटिश साम्राज्य (British Empire) वे देश तथा भूमियाँ थी जिन पर पहले ब्रिटेन द्वारा अफ्रीका, केरेबियन, उत्तरी अमेरिका, एशिया तथा ऑस्ट्रेलिया में उपनिवेश बनाए गए थे
By-election	उपचुनाव (By-election) ऐसा चुनाव है जो किसी निर्वाचन क्षेत्र के प्रतिनिधि की मृत्यु होने या त्यागपत्र देने पर फिर से कराया जाता है
Cabinet	मंत्रिमंडल (Cabinet) लगभग 20 सरकारी मंत्रियों की एक समिति होती है, जिसकी अध्यक्षता प्रधानमंत्री करते हैं, और वह सरकारी की नीति तय करने के लिए हर सप्ताह मिलती है
Canvas	प्रचार (Canvas) ऐसी गतिविधि है जिसमें दूसरे का समर्थन माँगा जाता है, विशेष रूप से चुनाव में मतदाताओं से
Census	जनगणना (Census) एक सरकारी सर्वेक्षण है जो प्रत्येक 10 वर्ष में आयोजित किया जाता हैं जो सभी निवासियों द्वारा पूर्ण किया जाना चाहिए
Chancellor of the Exchequer	वित्त मंत्री (The Chancellor of the Exchequer) आर्थिक नीति के लिए उत्तरदायी मंत्री होता है
Civil Service	प्रशासनिक सेवा (Civil Service) स्वतंत्र प्रबंधक और प्रशासक होते हैं जो सरकारी नीति को लागू करते हैं
Cockney	कॉकने (Cockney) लंदन में रहने वाले लोगों का प्रादेशिक लहज़ा है
Commonwealth	राष्ट्रकुल (Commonwealth) एक अंतर्राष्ट्रीय संगठन है जिसके 54 सदस्य देश हैं, इसका उद्भव ब्रिटिश साम्राज्य के अवशेषों से हुआ है
Constituency	निर्वाचन क्षेत्र (Constituency) चुनाव में प्रयोग में आने वाला एक स्थानीय क्षेत्र होता है। लोग लोकसभा (हाउस ऑफ कॉमन्स) में उनके निर्वाचन क्षेत्र का प्रतिनिधित्व करने के लिए किसी व्यक्ति को मत देते हैं
Constitution	संविधान (Constitution) किसी देश का शासन किस प्रकार किया जाए उसके नियमों का एक समुच्चय है
Controlled drugs	नियंत्रित दवाएँ (Controlled drugs) अवैध दवाएँ हैं जैसे हेरोइन कोकीन, एक्सटेसी, और गांजा

Convention	परम्परा (Convention) कोई नियम या रिवाज़ है जो सामान्यतः अलिखित होते हैं
Coronation	राज्याभिषेक (Coronation) एक समारोह है जो नए राजा या रानी को राजगद्दी पर बिठाए जाने पर मनाया जाता है
Council of Europe	यूरोप परिषद (Council of Europe) 50 यूरोपियन राज्यों से मिलकर बनी है। ये मानवाधिकारों का संरक्षण तथा यूरोपियन समस्याओं के उपाय ढूँढ़ने के लिए कार्य करती है
Council of Ministers	मंत्रि परिषद् (Council of Ministers) EU देशों के मंत्रियों से मिल कर बनी है। ये नए नियम प्रस्तावित करती है तथा EU उन किस प्रकार चले उसका निर्णय करती है
Denomination	पंथ (denomination) किसी धर्म विशिष्ट की शाखा होती है। उदाहरण के लिए ईसाई संप्रदाय का एक पंथ एंग्लिकन चर्च है
Devolved administration	सुपर्द प्रशासन (Devolved administration) यह सिद्धांत है जिसके तहत केंद्रीय सरकार अपनी शक्तियां प्रादेशिक निकायों को देती है। इसलिए कभी कभी इसे 'होम रूल' कहते हैं क्योंकि इसका अर्थ है कि कुछ सरकारी निर्णय प्रादेशिक संसदों द्वारा लिए जाते हैं, जैसे वेल्स की विधान सभा।
Divorce	तलाक़ (Divorce) विवाह का कानूनी अंत
Easter eggs	ईस्टर अंडे (Easter eggs) चाकलेट अंडे हैं जो ईस्टर पर उपहार के रूप में दिए जाते हैं
Electoral Register	मत सूची रजिस्टर (electoral register) चुनाव में मतदान करने के पात्र सभी लोगों की सूची हैं
European Commission	यूरोपियन आयोग (European Commission) ब्रुसेल्स में स्थित एक संगठन है, जो EU की गतिविधियों को चलाने के लिए उत्तरदायी है
European Economic Community	युरोपियन आर्थिक समुदाय (European Economic Community) EU का पुराना नाम।
European Union (EU)	यूरोपीय संघ (EU) 25 सदस्य राज्यों का एक संगठन। इसमें सदस्य सहायता करते हैं, विशेष कर आर्थिक मामलों में।
Father Christmas	फ़ादर क्रिसमस (Father Christmas) पौराणिक पात्र है, जो क्रिसमस पर बच्चों को उपहार बाँटता है
First Past the Post	फ़र्स्ट पास्ट द पोस्ट (First Past the Post) निर्वाचन प्रणाली है जो UK में प्रयोग में लाई जाती है

Football Association (FA)	फुटबॉल एसोसिएशन (The Football Association (FA)) इंग्लैंड में फुटबॉल खेल को चलाने के लिए उत्तरदायी होता है
Foreign Secretary	विदेश मंत्री (Foreign Secretary) वो मंत्री है जो विदेशी नीति तथा ब्रिटेन के अन्य देशों के साथ संबध बनाने के लिए उत्तरदायी होता है
Free press	फ्री प्रेस (Free press) का अर्थ है ब्रिटेन का मीडिया जो सरकार द्वारा नियंत्रित नहीं होता है
Gaelic	गीलिक (Gaelic) स्कॉटलैन्ड की मूल भाषा है
GCSE	सामान्य माध्यमिक शिक्षा प्रमाणपत्र (General Certificate of Secondary Education (GCSE)) का संक्षिप्त रूप जो 16 वर्ष की आयु के विद्यार्थियों के लिए निश्चित किया गया है
General Election	आम चुनाव (General Election) प्रत्येक पाँच वर्ष में हाउस ऑफ कॉमन्स के सदस्यों के निर्वाचन के लिए आयोजित किया जाता हैं
Geordie	ज्योर्डी (Geordie) टाउनसाईड या न्यू केसल ऑन टाइन में रहने वालों लोगों का प्रादेशिक लहज़ा है
Grand National	ग्रैण्ड नेशनल (Grand National) वर्ष में एक बार अप्रैल में आयोजित की जाने वाली एक घुड़दौड़ है
Gunpowder Plot	गन पावर प्लॉट में (Gunpowder Plot) में 1605 में साज़िश करने वालों का एक समूह शामिल थे जो संसद के सदनों को उड़ाने की योजना बना रहे थे
Guy Fawkes Night	गाई फ़ॉक्स नाईट (Guy Fawkes Night) गन पावडर प्लॉट को नाकाम करने के समारोह के रूप में प्रतिवर्ष आयोजित किया जाता हैं
Hansard	हैंसर्ड (Hansard) संसद की कार्यवाही का सरकारी रेकार्ड है
Hard drugs	कठोर दवाइयाँ (Hard drugs) नियंत्रित दवाओं का अति गंभीर रूप हैं, जैसे हेरोइन तथा कोकीन
Hereditary Peers	वंशानुगत कुलीन (Hereditary Peers) हाउस ऑफ लॉर्ड्स में होते थे। वे अपने पद उनके माता पिता से विरासत में प्राप्त करते थे
Home Secretary	गृह मंत्री (Home Secretary) कानून एवं परिस्थिति एवं आप्रवासन के लिए उत्तरदायी मंत्री होता है

House of Commons	हाउस ऑफ कॉमन्स (House of Commons) संसद का निम्न सदन होता। है
House of Lords	हाउस ऑफ लॉर्ड्स (House of Lords) संसद का उच्च सदन होता है
Houses of Parliament	संसद के सदन (Houses of Parliament) हाउस ऑफ कॉमन्स तथा हाउस ऑफ लॉर्ड्स दोनों को परिभाषित करने के लिए प्रयोग किया जाता है।
Independent candidate	निर्दलीय उम्मीदवार (independent candidate) एक ऐसा व्यक्ति हैं जो संसद में चुना जाता हैं, पर किसी राजनैतिक पार्टी से जुडा नहीं होता है।
Iron Curtain	लोहे का पर्दा (Iron Curtain) पश्चिमी तथा पूर्वीय विश्व को पृथक करने वाली एक आभासी रेखा को कहते थे जो 1980 में सोवियत संघ के पतन तक थी
Kirk	कर्क (Kirk) प्रेस्बिटेरियन गिरजे (स्काटलैण्ड गिरजे) का एक वैकल्पिक नाम है
Leader of the Opposition	विपक्ष के नेता (Leader of the Opposition) संसद में दूसरी बड़ी पार्टी के नेता होता है
Legislation	विधि (Legislation) सभी कानूनों के लिए एक सामान्य नाम दिया गया है
Life Peers	आजीवन कुलीन (Life Peers) प्रधानमंत्री द्वारा नियुक्त व्यक्ति जो हाउस ऑफ लॉर्ड्स में बैठता हैं।
Lord Chancellor	न्याय मंत्री (Lord Chancellor) सरकारी मंत्री होता हैं जो नए न्यायाधीशों की नियुक्ति के लिए उत्तरदायी होता है
Lower House	निम्न सदन (Lower House) एक संसद हैं जो नीतियों तथा कानून के बारे में निर्णय लेते हैं। युनाईटेड किंगडम निम्न सदन हाउस ऑफ कॉमन्स है
Member of Parliament (MP)	संसद सदस्य (Member of Parliament (MP)) एक लोक प्रतिनिधि है जिसे हाउस ऑफ कॉमन्स में बैठने के लिए निर्वाचित किया जाता है
Metropolitan Police	मेट्रोपोलीटन पुलिस (Metropolitan Police) लंदन के लोगों की सेवा करने वाला पुलिस बल है
Middle ground	मध्य आधार (Middle ground) दो विरोधी विचार–धाराओं के बीच मध्य बिंदु पर सहमति है

Minister	मंत्री (Minister) एक वरिष्ठ सरकारी राजनीतिज्ञ होता है जिसके नीतियों संबंधी तथा अन्य उत्तरदायित्व हैं
Monarch	मोनार्क (Monarch) राजा या रानी होते हैं
Mothering Sunday	मदरिंग सण्डे (Mothering Sunday) समारोह का एक दिन होता है जिसमे बच्चे अपनी माताओं की सराहना करते हैं
Mugging	मगिंग (Mugging) गलियों में धमकी या हिंसा से चोरी करने का अपराध
National Assembly for Wales	वेल्स राष्ट्रीय सभा (National Assembly for Wales) जहाँ वेल्स के प्रतिनिधि नीति के मामलों को जानने के लिए मिलते है। ये कार्डिफ़ में स्थित है
National Day	राष्ट्रीय दिवस (National Day), जैसे सेंट पेट्रिक दिवस, किसी देश और उसके गठन के लिए मनाया जाता है।
New Scotland Yard	न्यू स्काटलैण्ड यार्ड (New Scotland Yard) मेट्रोपोलिटन पुलिस का मुख्यालय है
Non-departmental Public Bodies	गैर–विभागीय सार्वजनिक निकाय (Non-departmental Public Bodies) सरकार द्वारा स्थापित एवं फन्डेड एजेंसियाँ है। उनके पास सरकारी विभागों से ज़्यादा स्वायत्तता होती है और उन्हें बनाने वाले मंत्रियों या विभागों के सीधे नियंत्रण के बिना उन्हें संचालन करने दिया जाता है
Palace of Westminster	पैलेस ऑफ़ वेस्टमिन्स्टर (Palace of Westminster) में हाउस ऑफ़ कॉमन्स तथा हाउस ऑफ लॉर्ड्स स्थित हैं
Parliament	संसद (Parliament) जहाँ निर्वाचित राष्ट्रीय प्रतिनिधि मुद्दों तथा विकास नियमों पर चर्चा करने के लिए मिलते हैं
Parliament of Scotland	स्काटलैण्ड की संसद (Parliament of Scotland) एडिनबर्ग में स्थित है, तथा स्कॉटिश लोगों का प्रतिनिधित्व करती है।
Parliamentary Democracy	संसदीय लोकतंत्र (Parliamentary Democracy) एक ऐसा देश जहाँ सरकार के निर्णय प्रतिनिधियों की संसद द्वारा लिए जाते हैं
Party system	दल प्रणाली (Party system) एक राजनैतिक प्रणाली है जिसमें प्रतिनिधि तथा मतदाता स्वयं एक समूह में एकत्रित होते है। इन समूहों में सामान्यतः साझा मूल्य एवं ध्येय होते हैं
Presbyterian Church	प्रेस्बिटेरियन चर्च (Presbyterian Church) स्काटलैन्ड का गिरजाघर है

Pressure Groups	दबाव समूह (Pressure groups) जो विशिष्ट हितों वाले समूह होते हैं जो राजनैतिज्ञों को प्रभावित करने का प्रयास करते हैं
Prime Minister	प्रधानमंत्री शासन दल का नेता तथा मंत्रि मंडल का अध्यक्ष होता है
Proportional Representation	समानुपातिक प्रतिनिधित्व (Proportional Representation) एक निर्वाचन प्रणाली है जहाँ संसद की सीटें पार्टियों को प्राप्त मतों के अनुपात के आधार पर आवंटित की जाती हैं।
Protestant	प्रोटेस्टेंट (Protestant) ऐसा व्यक्तित्व जो ईसाई धर्म का अनुयायी होता है। इसमें एंग्लिकन चर्च तथा प्रेस्बिटेरियन चर्च के अनुयायी शामिल हैं
Quango	कवांगो (Quango) गैर विभागीय जन निकाय का दूसरा नाम है
Queen's Speech	महारानी का भाषण (Queen's Speech) सरकार की नीतियों तथा मंशाओं का संसद के नए सत्र के प्रारंभ महारानी द्वारा दिया गया भाषण
Question time	प्रश्न काल (Question time) लोकसभा में नियमित रूप से आवंटित समय है जिसमें सांसद मंत्रीयों से प्रश्न पूछ सकते है
Reformation	पूनःनिर्माण (Reformation) सोलहवीं शती का एक आंदोलन था जिसमें प्रोटेस्टेंटवाद को ब्रिटेन में स्थापित धर्म निश्चित किया गया
Remembrance Day	स्मरण दिवस (Remembrance Day) युद्ध में शहीदों के स्मरण में प्रत्येक नवंबर को आयोजित किया जाता है
Scouse	स्काउस (Scouse) लिवरपूल में रहने वाले लोगों का प्रादेशिक लहज़ा है।
Shadow Cabinet	छद्म मंत्रिमंडल (Shadow Cabinet) में मुख्य विपक्ष दल के सांसदों का एक समूह होता है जो महत्वपूर्ण मुद्दों पर संसद मे दल के प्रतिनिधित्व के लिए उतरदायी होते हैं
Speaker	अध्यक्ष (Speaker) हाउस ऑफ़ कॉमन्स तथा हाउस ऑफ़ लॉर्ड्स दोनों में संसदीय चर्चाओं में अध्यक्ष के रूप कार्य करते है
Spin	स्पिन (Spin) राजनैतिक पार्टियों के प्रवक्ताओं द्वारा जारी दृष्टिकोण।
St Andrew's Day	स्कॉटलैण्ड का राष्ट्रीय दिवस
St David's Day	वेल्स का राष्ट्रीय दिवस
St George's Day	इंग्लैण्ड का राष्ट्रीय दिवस

St Patrick's Day	उत्तरी आयरलैण्ड तथा आयरलैण्ड गणतंत्र का राष्ट्रीय दिवस
St Valentine's Day	सेंट वेलेन्टाइन दिवस (St Valentine's day) प्रत्येक फरवरी में प्यार तथा संबंघो के लिए मनाया जाता है
Stepfamily	जब बच्चों सहित लोग पुन:विवाह करते है तो सौतेला परिवार (stepfamily) बनता है।
Stormont	स्टोरमोंट (Stormont) उत्तरी आयरलैन्ड संसद का वैकल्पिक नाम है
Supreme Governor	सर्वोच्च राज्यपाल (Supreme Governor) एंग्लिकन चर्च के प्रमुख रूप में राजा द्वारा अदा की जाने वाली भूमिका है।
Treasury	ट्रेज़री (Treasury) सरकार के पास आने वाले, संग्रहित तथा खर्च किए जाने वाले तमाम धन के प्रबंघन के उत्तरदायी सरकारी विभाग हैं।
United Nations (UN)	संयुक्त राष्ट्र (United Nations (UN)) शांति, सुरक्षा तथा मानवाधिकारो को समर्पित एक वैश्विक संगठन
United Nations Security Council	संयुक्त राष्ट्र सुरक्षा परिषद 15 सदस्यों की एक समिति है जो वैश्विक सुरक्षा पर घ्यान रखती है। UK पाँच स्थाई सदस्यों में से एक है
Upper House	ऊच्च सदन (Upper House) नीतियों तथा कानून के निर्णयों की समीक्षा करने वाली संसद है। युनाईटेड किंगडम में हाउस ऑफ लॉर्ड्स ऊपरी सदन है
Westminster	वेस्टमिन्स्टर (Westminster) एक सामान्य शब्द है जो सरकार के बारे में प्रयोग किया जाता है।
Whips	व्हिप वे सांसद है जो यह सुनिश्चित करते हैं उनकी पार्टी के अन्य सांसद पार्टी के मंतव्यो के अनुसार मत दें।
Wimbledon	विम्बल्डन (Wimbledon) दक्षिण लंदन में सालाना आयोजित किया जाने वाला एक सम्मानीय टेनिस टूर्नामेंट है

الفاظ جو معلوم ہونے چاہئیں

ذیل میں ان اصطلاحات کی فہرست دی جارہی ہے جن کا استعمال سرکاری مطالعاتی مواد میں ہوتا ہے۔ آپ کو یوکے کے امتحانات میں شرکت کے لئے کچھ اصطلاحات کے معنی معلوم ہونے چاہئیں۔ دیگر اصطلاحات کو پس منظر کی معلومات کے طور پر شامل کیا گیا ہے تاکہ آپ مطالعاتی رہنما کے کچھ اہم تصورات اور حقائق سے آگاہ ہو سکیں۔

برطانوی وزیر اعظم کی سرکاری رہائش گاہ	10 Downing Street
سطح اے (لیول A) وہ امتحانات ہیں جو طلباء اپنے اسکول کے آخری سال میں دیتے ہیں جب کہ ان کی عمر 18 سال کی ہوتی ہے	A Levels
سطح اے/ ایس (لیول A/S) وہ امتحانات ہیں جو طلبا اسکول میں اپنے دوسرے سال سے لے کر آخری سال تک دیتے ہیں، جب کہ ان کی عمر 17 سال کی ہوتی ہے	A/S Levels
منسوخی کسی چیز کے اختتام کو کہتے ہیں، جیسے کہ کوئی عمل یا روایت	Abolition
عمردراز آبادی ایسی آبادی ہے جہاں اوسط عمر بڑھ رہی ہو۔ یہ عام طور پر شرح پیدائش میں کمی یا طویل دور حیات کے سبب ہوتا ہے	Aging population
اینگلیکن چرچ کو انگلینڈ کا چرچ بھی کہا جاتا ہے	Anglican Church
اپریل کا یوم مذاق، ماہ اپریل کے پہلے دن ہوتا ہے۔ لوگ ایک دوسرے کے ساتھ مذاق کرکے اس دن کا لطف لیتے ہیں	April Fool's Day
کنٹربری کے آرک بشپ اینگلیکن چرچ کے سربراہ ہوتے ہیں	Archbishop of Canterbury
بینک تعطیلات وہ سرکاری چھٹیاں ہوتی ہیں جن میں بینک اور زیادہ تر کاروبار کو بند ہونا چاہئے	Bank holidays
بلانوشی زیادہ مقدار میں شراب پینے کو کہتے ہیں۔ حالیہ سالوں کے دوران یہ عوامی بدنظمی اور چھوٹے موٹے جرائم سے متعلق تشویش کا مرکز بن گیا ہے	Binge drinking
بشپ عیسائی چرچ کا سب سے بڑا پادری ہوتا ہے	Bishop
گھر سے باہر جلائی جانے والی بڑی اور روشن آگ جسے کسی تقریب کے موقع پر جلایا جاتا ہے۔ خاص کر گیے فوکس نائٹ پر	Bonfire
باکسنگ ڈے کا انعقاد 26 دسمبر کو کیا جاتا ہے۔ روایتی طور پر اس دن لوگ نوکروں، مالیوں اور دیگر کام کرنے والوں کو تحفے دیتے تھے	Boxing Day

کونسل آف یوروپ 50 یوروپی ممالک پر مشتمل ہے۔ یہ حقوق انسانی کے تحفظ اور یوروپی مسائل کا حل نکالنے کے لئے کام کرتی ہے	Council of Europe
وزراء کی کابینہ یوروپین یونین کی ریاستوں کے وزراء پر مشتمل ہوتی ہے۔ یہ نئے قوانین تجویز کرتی ہے اور یوروپین یونین کو چلانے کے طریقوں کے بارے میں فیصلے کرتی ہے	Council of Ministers
فرقہ کسی مذہب کا ایک مخصوص شاخ ہوتا ہے۔ مثال کے طور پر، اینگلیکن چرچ عیسائیت کا ایک فرقہ ہے	Denomination
انتظامی امور کی تفویض، مرکزی حکومت کا ایک اصول ہے جس کے تحت وہ علاقائی انتظامیہ کو اختیارات فراہم کرتی ہے۔ کبھی کبھی اسے 'داخلی ضابطہ' بھی کہتے ہیں جس کا مطلب یہ ہوتا ہے کہ حکومت کے بعض مخصوص امور کے بارے میں علاقائی مجلسوں کے ذریعہ فیصلہ لیا جا سکتا ہے، جیسے اسمبلی برائے ویلز	Devolved administration
طلاق، شادی کا قانونی طور پر خاتمہ ہوتا ہے	Divorce
عیدالفصح (ایسٹر) کے موقع پر تحفتاً دی جانے والی بیضوی شکل کی مٹھائی یا چاکلیٹ	Easter eggs
چناوی فہرست (انتخابی فہرست) الکشن میں ووٹ دینے کے مستحق افراد کی فہرست ہوتی ہے	Electoral Register
یوروپین کمیشن، بروسیلس میں واقع ایک تنظیم ہے جو یوروپین یونین کی سرگرمیوں کی انجام دہی کے لئے ذمہ دار ہے	European Commission
یوروپین یونین کا پرانا نام ہے	European Economic Community
25 ممبر ممالک کی ایک تنظیم ہے۔ اس کے ذریعہ ممبران کو خاص طور پر اقتصادی معاملات میں باہم تعاون کا موقع ملتا ہے	European Union (EU)
فادر کرسمس ایک روایتی کردار ہے جو کرسمس کے موقع پر بچوں میں تحفے تقسیم کرتا ہے	Father Christmas
فرسٹ پاسٹ دی پوسٹ برطانیہ (یوکے) میں استعمال ہونے والا انتخابی نظام ہے	First Past the Post
فٹبال ایسوسیشن، انگلینڈ میں فٹبال کے کھیل سے متعلق امور کی انجام دہی کے لئے ذمہ دار ہے	Football Association (FA)
وزیر خارجہ، وہ وزیر ہے جو خارجہ پالیسی اور دوسرے ممالک کے ساتھ برطانیہ کے تعلقات کے لئے ذمہ دار ہے	Foreign Secretary

برطانوی سامراج میں وہ ممالک اور خطے شامل تھے جن کی نوآبادکاری برطانیہ نے افریقہ، کریبین، شمالی امریکہ، ایشیا اور آسٹریلیا میں کی تھی	British Empire
ضمنی انتخاب ایک ایسا انتخاب ہے جس کا انعقاد اس وقت ہوتا ہے جب کہ کسی مخصوص حلقے کے نمائندے کی موت ہوجاتی ہے یا وہ مستعفی ہو جاتا ہے	By-election
کابینہ حکومت کے لگ بھگ 20 وزراء کی ایک کمیٹی ہوتی ہے، جس کا سربراہ وزیر اعظم ہوتا ہے، جو ہفتہ واری طور پر سرکار کی پالیسی کے بارے میں فیصلہ کرنے کے لئے میٹنگ کرتے ہیں	Cabinet
رائے ہموار کرنے کا مطلب ہے سرگرمی کے ساتھ کسی کی اعانت حاصل کرنا، خاص کر انتخابات کے دوران ووٹر کی	Canvas
مردم شماری سرکار کے ذریعہ کیا جانے والا سروے ہے جو ہر 10 سال پر کیا جاتا ہے، اور اس میں تمام باشندوں کو شامل کرنا ضروری ہے	Census
وزیر برائے محصولات، اقتصادی پالیسیوں کے لئے ذمہ دار وزیر ہوتا ہے	Chancellor of the Exchequer
سرکار کی شہری خدمات، میں خودمختار منتظمین اور ناظم ہوتے ہیں جو سرکار کی پالیسیوں پر عمل درآمد کرواتے ہیں	Civil Service
کاکنی، لندن میں رہنے والے لوگوں کا علاقائی لہجہ	Cockney
دولت مشترکہ ایک بین الاقوامی تنظیم ہے جس میں 54 ریاستیں شامل ہیں۔ یہ ماضی کی برطانوی سلطنت کے بقایا جات سے بنی ہے	Commonwealth
حلقہ، انتخابات کے لئے مقرر ایک مقامی علاقہ ہوتا ہے۔ لوگ ایوان زیریں میں اپنے حلقے کی نمائندگی کے لئے ایک شخص کا انتخاب کرتے ہیں	Constituency
دستور، ملک کو چلانے سے متعلق ضابطوں کا ایک مجموعہ ہوتا ہے	Constitution
ممنوعہ منشیات، غیرقانونی دوائیں ہوتی ہیں جیسے ہیروئین، کوکین، ایکسٹیسی، کینابیس	Controlled drugs
رواج، ایسے اصول یا روایات ہوتے ہیں جو عام طور پر غیر تحریر شدہ ہوتے ہیں	Convention
تاج پوشی، ایک ایسی تقریب ہے جس میں نئے شہنشاہ کو حکومت کی باگ ڈور سونپا جاتا ہے	Coronation

آہنی پردہ، اس خیالی لکیر کی وضاحت کرتا ہے جو 1980 میں سوویت یونین کے تحلیل ہونے سے پہلے مغربی اور مشرقی دنیا کو الگ کرتی تھی	Iron Curtain
کرک، پریسبیٹیرین چرچ (اسکاٹ لینڈ کے چرچ) کا ایک متبادل نام ہے	Kirk
حزب اختلاف کا قائد، پارلیامنٹ کی دوسری سب سے بڑی پارٹی کا قائد ہوتا ہے	Leader of the Opposition
وضع قوانین، تمام قوانین کے لئے استعمال ہونے والی ایک اصطلاح	Legislation
لائف پیئرز، وزیر اعظم کے ذریعہ ایوان بالا (دار الامراء) میں نامزد کیے جانے والے اراکین ہوتے ہیں	Life Peers
لارڈ چانسلر، نئے ججوں کا تقرر کرنے کے لئے ذمہ دار حکومت کا وزیر ہوتا ہے	Lord Chancellor
ایوان زیریں، پارلیامنٹ کا وہ حصہ ہے جو پالیسی اور قوانین کے بارے میں فیصلے کرتا ہے۔ برطانیہ (یوکے) میں ایوان زیریں کو دارالعوام (ہاؤس آف کامنز) بھی کہا جاتا ہے	Lower House
رکن پارلیامنٹ، عوام کا نمائندہ ہوتا ہے جسے ایوان زیریں کے لئے منتخب کیا جاتا ہے	Member of Parliament (MP)
میٹروپولیٹین پولیس وہ پولیس فورس ہے جو لندن کے لوگوں کی خدمت کرتی ہے	Metropolitan Police
درمیانی راستہ (مڈل گراؤنڈ) دو مختلف نظریات کے درمیان اتفاق کا نکتہ ہے	Middle ground
وزیر، پالیسیوں اور دیگر ذمے داریوں کا حامل ایک اعلی سرکاری سیاستداں ہوتا ہے	Minister
شہنشاہ، ملکہ یا بادشاہ کے لئے مستعمل ہے	Monarch
یوم مادر، اتوار کو منایا جانے والا دن ہے جس میں بچے اپنی ماں کو خراج تہنیت پیش کرتے ہیں	Mothering Sunday
سڑکوں پر دھماکہ یا تشدد کرکے سامان لوٹ لینے کا مجرمانہ عمل	Mugging
ویلز کی قومی اسمبلی، میں ویلز کے نمائندے پالیسی کے تعین کے لئے جمع ہوتے ہیں۔ یہ کارڈیف میں واقع ہے	National Assembly for Wales
قومی دن، جیسے سینٹ پیٹرکس ڈے، جسے پورا ملک اپنے یوم تاسیس کے طور پر مناتا ہے	National Day
نیو اسکاٹ لینڈ یارڈ، میٹروپولیٹین پولیس کا صدر دفتر ہے	New Scotland Yard

آزاد پریس کا مطلب یہ ہے کہ برطانیہ میں، ذرائع ابلاغ حکومت کے ماتحت نہیں ہیں	Free press
گیلک، اسکاٹ لینڈ کی مقامی زبان ہے	Gaelic
ثانوی تعلیم کی عمومی سند (جنرل سرٹیفکٹ آف سیکنڈری ایجوکیشن) کا مخفف ہے۔ طلبا 16 سال کی عمر میں جی سی ایس ای امتحانات میں بیٹھتے ہیں	GCSE
عام انتخابات کا انعقاد ہر پانچ سال پر ایوان زیریں کے نمائندوں کے انتخاب کے لئے کیا جاتا ہے	General Election
جیورڈائی، ٹائن سائڈ یا نیوکیسل اپ آن ٹائن میں رہنے والوں کا مقامی لہجہ ہے	Geordie
گرانڈ نیشنل، ایک گھڑ دوڑ ہے جس کا انعقاد ہرسال ایک بار اپریل میں کیا جاتا ہے	Grand National
بارودی سازش (گن پاؤڈر پلاٹ)، 1605 میں ہونے والی اس سازش میں سازشیوں کے ایک گروہ نے پارلیا منٹ ہاؤس کو اڑانے کی سازش کی تھی	Gunpowder Plot
گیے فوکس نائٹ ہرسال بارودی سازش (گن پاؤڈر پلاٹ) کے انسداد کی یاد میں منایا جاتا ہے	Guy Fawkes Night
ہنسرڈ، پارلیمنٹ کی تمام سرگرمیوں کا ریکارڈ ہوتا ہے	Hansard
خطرناک منشیات، ممنوعہ منشیات کی خطرناک ترین قسم ہوتی ہے، جیسے ہیروئین اور کوکین	Hard drugs
ہیریڈیٹری پیئرس (موروثی رکن) ایوان بالا (دارالامرا) کی تشکیل کرتے ہیں۔ انھیں اپنے والدین سے موروثی طور پر یہ منصب حاصل ہوتا ہے	Hereditary Peers
وزیر داخلہ، وہ وزیر ہوتا ہے جو قانون و انتظام اور امیگریشن کے امور کا ذمہ دار ہوتا ہے	Home Secretary
ایوان زیریں پارلیامنٹ کی زیریں اسمبلی ہوتی ہے	House of Commons
ایوان بالا (دارالامرا) پارلیامنٹ کی اعلی اسمبلی ہوتی ہے	House of Lords
ہاؤس آف پارلیامنٹ کا استعمال ایوان زیریں اور ایوان بالا (دارالامرا) کو مشترکہ طور پر بیان کرنے کے لئے کیا جاتا ہے	Houses of Parliament
آزاد امیدوار، وہ شخص ہوتا ہے جو پارلیامنٹ کے لئے منتخب ہونے کی کوشش کرتا ہے، لیکن وہ کسی سیاسی پارٹی سے وابستہ نہیں ہوتا	Independent candidate

وقفہ سوالات، ایوان زیریں میں ایک مقررہ وقفہ ہے جس میں ممبران پارلیامنٹ (MPs)، وزراء سے سوالات پوچھ سکتے ہیں	Question time
ریفارمیشن (اصلاح کلیسا)، سولہویں صدی کی ایک تحریک تھی جس نے پروٹسٹنٹ ازم کو برطانیہ کے مذہب کے طور پر مستحکم کردیا	Reformation
یادگار دن، ہر سال نومبر میں جنگ میں مرنے والوں کی یاد میں منایا جانے والا دن	Remembrance Day
اسکاؤز، لیورپول کے لوگوں کا علاقائی لہجہ ہے	Scouse
فرضی کابینہ، پارلیامنٹ میں اصل حزب اختلاف کے ایسے ممبران پارلیامنٹ کی ایک جماعت، جو اہم معاملات پر پارٹی کی نمائندگی کے لئے ذمہ دار ہو	Shadow Cabinet
اسپیکر، ایوان زیریں اور ایوان بالا دونوں میں پارلیمانی مباحثوں کے دوران صدر کی حیثیت سے کام کرتا ہے	Speaker
اسپن، نقطہ نظر سے متعلق تبصرہ ہوتا ہے، جس کا اظہار سیاسی پارٹیوں کے ترجمان کسی معاملے پر کرتے ہیں	Spin
اسکاٹ لینڈ کا قومی دن	St Andrew's Day
ویلز کا کا قومی دن	St David's Day
انگلینڈ کا کا قومی دن	St George's Day
شمالی آئر لینڈ اور جمہوریہ آئرلینڈ کا کا قومی دن	St Patrick's Day
سینٹ ویلنٹائنز ڈے، ہر سال فروری میں محبت اور رشتوں کی یاد میں منایا جاتا ہے	St Valentine's Day
سوتیلا خاندان، ایسی صورت میں بنتا ہے جب بچے والے لوگ دوسری شادی کرلیتے ہیں	Stepfamily
اسٹارمونٹ، شمالی آئرلینڈ کی پارلیامنٹ کا متبادل نام ہے	Stormont
سپریم گورنر (مقتدر اعلیٰ) شہنشاہ کے ذریعہ انجام دیا جانے والا کردار ہے جیسے کہ اینگلیکن چرچ کا سربراہ	Supreme Governor
ٹریزری (خزانہ) حکومت کا ایک محکمہ ہے جو حکومت کو حاصل ہونے والے، اس کے پاس جمع، اور خرچ ہونے والے تمام رقوم کے انتظام و انصرام کا ذمہ دار ہے۔	Treasury
اقوام متحدہ، ایک عالمی تنظیم ہے جو امن، تحفظ اور حقوق انسانی کے لئے وقف ہے	United Nations (UN)

غیر محکمہ جاتی سرکاری ادارے ایسی ایجنسیاں ہیں جن کی تشکیل اور فنڈ کی فراہمی حکومت کے ذریعہ ہوتی ہے۔ انہیں حکومت کے محکموں سے زیادہ آزادی حاصل ہوتی ہے اور عام طور پر انہیں ان وزراء یا محکموں کے براہ راست تسلط سے آزاد ہوکر کام کرنے کا اختیار ہوتا ہے جو ان کی تشکیل کرتے ہیں	Non-departmental Public Bodies
ویسٹ منسٹر کا محل، ایوان زیریں اور ایوان بالا کی عمارت ہے	Palace of Westminster
پارلیامنٹ، وہ مقام ہے جہاں منتخب قومی نمائندے معاملات پر بحث کرنے اور قانون کو ترقی دینے کے لئے جمع ہوتے ہیں	Parliament
ایڈنبرگ میں واقع اسکاٹ لینڈ کی پارلیامنٹ، اسکاٹ لینڈ کے باشندوں کی نمائندگی کرتی ہے	Parliament of Scotland
پارلیمانی جمہوریت، ایسے ملک کی وضاحت کرتی ہے جہاں حکومت کے فیصلے نمائندوں کے ایک پارلیامنٹ کے ذریعہ کیے جاتے ہیں	Parliamentary Democracy
پارٹی نظام، ایک سیاسی نظام ہے جس میں نمائندے اور ووٹر (رائے دہندگان) خود کو جماعتوں کی شکل میں منظم کرتے ہیں۔ عام طور پر ان جماعتوں کے مشترکہ نظریات اور نشانے ہوتے ہیں	Party system
پریسبیٹیرین چرچ، اسکاٹ لینڈ کا چرچ ہے	Presbyterian Church
دباؤ ڈالنے والی جماعتیں، خصوصی مفادات کی حامل جماعتیں ہوتی ہیں جو سیاست دانوں پر اپنا اثر ڈالتی ہیں	Pressure Groups
وزیر اعظم، حکمران پارٹی کا قائد اور کابینہ کا سربراہ ہوتا ہے	Prime Minister
تناسبی نمائندگی، ایک انتخابی نظام ہے جس میں حاصل ہونے والے ووٹ کے تناسب میں پارٹیوں کو پارلیامنٹ کی سیٹیں دی جاتی ہیں	Proportional Representation
پروٹسٹنٹ، عیسائی مذہب کے پیروکار کو کہتے ہیں۔ اس میں اینگلیکن چرچ اور پریسبیٹیرین چرچ کے پیروکار شامل ہیں	Protestant
کوانجو، غیر محکمہ جاتی سرکاری اداروں (نان ڈپارٹمنٹل پبلک ہاڈی) کا دوسرا نام ہے	Quango
ملکہ کی تقریر، ملکہ کے ذریعہ پارلیامنٹ کے نئے اجلاس کی ابتداء کے موقع پر پیش کی جاتی ہے جس میں حکومت کی پالیسیوں اور ارادوں کا بیان ہوتا ہے	Queen's Speech

اقوام متحدہ کی سلامتی کونسل، 15 ممبران کی ایک کمیٹی ہے جو عالمی سلامتی پر مرکوز ہے۔ یوکے اس کے پانچ مستقل اراکین مین سے ایک ہے	United Nations Security Council
ایوان بالا، پارلیامنٹ کا وہ حصہ ہے جو پالیسی اور قوانین سے متعلق فیصلوں پر نظرثانی کرتا ہے۔ برطانیہ میں ایوان بالا، دارالامراء کو کہا جاتا ہے	Upper House
ویسٹ منسٹر، عام طور پر سرکار کے لئے استعمال کیا جانے والا لفظ ہے	Westminster
وھپس، ایسے ممبران پارلیامنٹ ہوتے ہیں جو یہ یقینی بناتے ہیں کہ ان کی سیاسی پارٹی کے دیگر ممبران پارلیامنٹ اپنا ووٹ پارٹی کے ارادوں کے مطابق ہی دیں	Whips
ومبلڈن ایک باوقار ٹینس ٹورنامنٹ ہے جس کا انعقاد ہرسال جنوبی لندن میں ہوتا ہے	Wimbledon

EREYADA LOO BAAHAN YAHAY IN LA OGAADO

Halkan hoose waxaa ku taxan ereyo qayb ka ah shayada rasmiga ah ee waxbarashada (official study materials). Waxaad u baahan doontaa in aad ogaato macnaha ereyada qaarkood si aad uga gudubto Imtixaanka Nolosha Ingiriiska (Life in the UK Test). Ereyo kale ayaa lagu daray iyagoo ah macluumaad asal ahaan khuseeya mawduuca kaana caawinaya fahanka qaar ka mid ah fikradaha guud iyo xaqiiqooyinka muhiimka ah ee ku jira hagaha waxbarashada.

10 Downing Street	Guriga rasmiga ah ee Ra'iisal Wasaaraha Ingiriiska
A Levels	A Levels waa imtixaannada ay maraan ardayda ku jirta sanadkooda dugsiga ugu dambeeya, marka ay 18 jir yihiin
A/S Levels	A/S Levels waa imtixaannada ay maraan ardayda ku jirta sanadkooda dugsiga ugu dambeeya ka ka horreeya, marka ay 17 jir yihiin
Abolition (Tirtiridda)	Tirtiriddu waa joojinta wax, caado ama dhaqan ah
Aging population (Shacabka gaboobaya)	Shacabka gaboobayaa waa ka da'diisa isku celceliska ahi ay kordhayso. Waxaa kan caadi ahaan sabab u ah dhalmooyinka tira yaraanaya iyo cimriga oo sii dheeraanaya
Madhabta Anglican Church	Madhabta Anglican Church waxaa kaloo loo yaqaannaa Church of England
April Fool's Day (Maalinta Kaftanka ee Abriil)	Maalinta Kaftanka ee Abriil waa maalinta koowaad ee bisha Abriil. Waxay dadku maalintaas ku xusaan kaftan ay isla galaan.
Wadaadka sare ee Archbishop of Canterbury	Wadaadka sare ee Archbishop of Canterbury waa madaxa madhabta Anglican Church
Bank holidays (Maalmaha fasaxa rasmiga ah)	Maalmaha fasaxa rasmiga ahi waa maalmaha dadweynuhu fasaxa yahay ee bangiyada iyo goobaha ganacsiga badidood ay waajib ku tahay in ay xirnaadaan
Binge drinking (Cabbitaanka xad dhaafka ah ee khamriga)	Cabbitaanka xad dhaafka ah ee khamriga waa marka aalkolada loo cabbo si xad dhaaf ah. Sanadahan dhow waxay taasi walaac weyn ku dhalisay qalaalasaha dadweynaha iyo dembiyada yar yar ee ka yimaadda

Bishop (Wadaadka kiristaanka)	Wadaadka kiristaanka waa qof kaalin sare ka haya kaniisadda Kiristaanka
Bonfire (Dab shid)	Dab weyn oo dibadda si maamulan looga shido oo loogu talagalay wixii xaflad ama xus ah - gaar ahaan Habeenka Guy Fawkes
Maalinta Boxing Day	Maalinta Boxing Day waxaa la xusaa 26ka Diseembar. Waxay dhaqan ahaan ahayd maalin dadku ay hadiyado siin jireen adeegeyaashooda, dadka beeraha uga shaqeeya iyo ganacsatada kale
British Empire (Waddamada Ingiriisku xukumi jiray)	Waddamada Ingiriisku xukumi jiray waa waddamadii iyo dhulalkii uu Ingiriisku ka gumaysan jiray Afrika, Kaarabiyanka, Waqooyiga Marakaynka, Aasiya iyo Australaasiya
By-election (Doorashada gaarka ah)	Doorashada gaarka ahi waa doorasho la qabto marka uu wakiilka degaan gaar ahi uu is casilo ama dhinto
Cabinet (Golaha wasiirrada)	Cabinet (Golaha wasiirrada) waa guddi ka kooban qiyaas ahaan 20 Wasiirro Dawli ah, oo uu guddoomiyo Ra'iisal Wasaaruhu, kuwaasoo kulma toddobaad kaste si ay u gooyaan siyaasadda Dawladda
Canvas (Wareegga qalqaalinta leh)	Samaynta wareegga qalqaalinta leh waa raadsashada firfircoonida leh ee taageerada dadka, gaar ahaan codbixiyeyaasha marka doorasho lagu jiro
Census (Tirakoobka)	Tirakoobku waa daraasad ay dawladdu 10kii sanaba mar qabato, taasoo deganeyaasha dhammaantood waajib ku ah in ay buuxiyaan
Chancellor of the Exchequer (Wasiirka Dhaqaalaha)	Wasiirka Dhaqaalaha waa Wasiirka u xilsaaran siyaasadda dhaqaalaha
Civil Service (Hay'adaha Dawladda)	Hay'adaha Dawladdu waa maamuleyaal iyo maareeyeyaal madaxbannaan oo hirgeliya siyaasadda Dawladda
Cockney	Cockney waa lahjadda goboleed ee ay ku hadlaan dadka London ku nool

Commonwealth (Darwaaqo sooranka)	Barwaaqo sooranku waa urur caalami ah oo 54 dal ay xubin ka yihiin. Waxa uu ka dhashay wixii ka haray Waddamada Ingiriisku xukumi jiray
Constituency (Degaanka)	Degaanku waa aag xaafadeed oo la isticmaalo marka doorashooyinka la qabanayo. Dadku waxay doortaan shakhsi degaankooda wakiil uga noqda Aqalka Komoniska
Constitution (Dastuurka)	Dastuurku waa xeerar u dejisan sida waddanka loo xukumo
Controlled drugs (Mukhaadaraadka)	Mukhaadaraadku waa daroogooyinka sharci darrada ah sida heriwiinta, kooka'iinta, ekstasida iyo xashiishadda
Convention (Dhaqan)	Dhaqanku waa xeer ama caado aanan badi qornayn
Coronation	Coronation waa xafladda la qabto marka Boqor ama boqorad cusub xukunka lagu wareejiyo
Council of Europe (Golaha Yurub)	Golaha Yurub waxa uu ka kooban yahay 50 dal oo Yurub ku yaalla. Waxuu ka shaqeeyaa dhowrista xuquuqda aadamaha waxuuna isku dayaa in uu xal u helo dhibaatooyinka Yurub ka taagan
Council of Ministers (Guddiga Wasiirrada)	Guddiga Wasiirradu waxuu ka kooban yahay Wasiirro ka kala socda dalalka Midowga Yurub. Waxuu soo jediyaa shuruuc cusub waxuuna go'aan ka gaaraa sida loo maamulo Midowga Yurub.
Denomination (Madhabta)	Madhabtu waa laan gaar ah oo diintu ay leedahay. Tusaale ahaan Anglican Church waa madhab diinta Kiristaanka ka tirsan
Devolved administration (Maamulka gobolaysan)	Maamulka gobolaysan waa mabda'a ay dawladda dhexe xukunkeeda ugu wareejinayso hay'adaha dawladda ee gobollada. Waxaa nidaamkaas mararka qaarkood loo yaqaannaa "Xeerka Guriga" (Home Rule) maadaama uu macnuhu yahay in arrimaha dawladda qaarkood ay go'aan ka gaari karaan baarlamaannada goboleed, sida Golaha Wales (Assembly for Wales)
Divorce (Furniinka)	Furniinku waa dhammaadka sharciga ah ee guurka
Easter eggs (Ukunnada ciidda listerka)	Ukunnada ciidda listerku waa shukulaatiyo ukun u eeg oo hadiyad ahaan loo bixiyo goorta ciidda listerka

Electoral Register (Diiwaanka Doorashooyinka)	Diiwaanka doorashooyinku waa liis ka kooban dhammaan dadka u qalma in ay ka codbixiyaan doorashooyinka
European Commission (Guddiga Yurub)	Guddiga Yurub waa ururka, saldhigiisu Brussels yahay, ee u xilsaaran maamulka hawlaha uu Midowga Yurub qabto
European Economic Community (Isbaahaysiga Dhaqaale ee Yurub)	Magacii hore ee Midowga Yurub
European Union (Midowga Yurub) (EU)	Urur ay 25 dal xubin ka yihiin. Waxuu xubnaha u fasaxaa wadashaqayn, ay gaar ahaan ka yeeshaan arrimaha dhaqaale
Father Christmas	Father Christmas waa qof quraafaad ah oo carruurta hadiyado siiya goorta Ciidda masiixiga
First Past the Post	First Past the Post waa nidaamka doorashooyinka ee Ingiriiska laga isticmaalo
Football Association (Ururka Kubbadda cagta)(FA)	Ururka Kubbadda cagtu ayaa u xilsaaran maamulka ciyaarta kubbadda cagta Ingland gudaheeda
Foreign Secretary (Wasiirka Arrimaha dibadda)	Wasiirka Arrimaha dibaddu waa Wasiirka u xilsaaran siyaasadda arrimaha dibadda iyo xiriirka uu Ingiriisku la leeyahay waddamada kale
Free press (Saxaafadda xorta ah)	Saxaafadda xorta ahi waxay ka dhigan tahay in warbaahinta Ingiriiska aysan Dawladdu xukumin
Gaelic	Gaelic waa luqadda dhaladka u ah Scotland
GCSE	Marka la soo gaabiyo General Certificate of Secondary Education (Shahaadada Guud ee Tacliinta Dhexe). Imtixaannada GCSE waxaa mara ardayda da'doodu ay 16 jir tahay
General Election (Doorashada Guud)	Doorashada Guud waxaa la qabtaa shantii sanaba mar si loo doorto xubnaha Aqalka Komoniska
Geordie	Geordie waa lahjadda goboleed ee ay ku hadlaan dadka ku nool Tyneside ama Newcastle upon Tyne
Grand National	Grand National waa tartan fardeed oo sanadkiiba mar la qabto bisha Abriil

Gunpowder Plot (Shirqoolka Baaruudda)	Shirqoolka Baaruudda ee 1605tii waxaa ku lug lahaa koox shirqool dhigeyaal ah oo Isku dayey in ay qarxiyaan Aqallada Baarlamaanka
Habeenka Guy Fawkes	Habeenka Guy Fawkes waxaa la qabtaa sanad kaste si loo xuso qallibidda Shirqoolka Baaruudda
Hansard	Hansard waa diiwaanka rasmiga ah ee dhammaan wixii ka dhaca baarlamaanka
Hard drugs (Mukhaadaraadka Ugu xun)	Mukhaadaraadka ugu xuni waa Mukhaadaraadka kuwa ugu daran, sida heriwiinta iyo kooka'iinta
Hereditary Peers (Xubnaha Dhaxalka ah ee aqalka duqayda)	Xubnaha dhaxalka ah ee aqalka duqaydu waxay fadhiisan jireen Aqalka duqayda. Waxay jagooyinkooda ka dhaxli jireen waalidiintood
Home Secretary (Wasiirka Arrimaha Gudaha)	Wasiirka Arrimaha Guduhu waa Wasiirka u xilsaaran sugidda sharciga iyo nidaamka iyo haajiraadda
House of Commons (Aqalka Komoniska)	Aqalka Komonisku waa golaha hoose ee baarlamaanka
House of Lords (Aqalka Duqayda)	Aqalka Duqaydu waa golaha sare ee baarlamaanka
Houses of Parliament (Aqallada Baarlamaanka)	Aqallada Baarlamaanka waxaa lagu tilmaamaa Aqalka Komoniska iyo Aqalka Duqayda labadoodaba
Independent candidate (Musharraxa madaxbannaan)	Musharraxa madaxbannaan waa qofka isku daya in loo doorto Baarlamaanka, ee aan laakiin ku jirin xisbi siyaasadeed
Iron Curtain (Siligga Adag)	Siligga Adagi waxuu tilmaamayaa xarriiqii khayaaliga ahaa ee u dhaxayn jiray qurbaha iyo waddamada bari ilaa iyo burburkii Midowga Ruushka (Soviet Union) dhammaadkii siddeetannadii
Kirk	Kirk waa magac kale oo lagu sheego Madhabta Presbyterian Church (Kaniisadda Scotland)
Leader of the Opposition (Hoggaamiyaha Mucaaradka)	Hoggaamiyaha Mucaaradku waa hoggaamiyaha xisbiga heerka labaad uga matalan baarlamaanka

Legislation (Qaanuunka)	Qaanuunku waa magaca guud ee lagu tilmaamo shuruucda dhammaantood
Life Peers (Xubnaha Cimriga ee Aqalka Duqayda)	Xubnaha Cimriga ee Aqalka Duqayda Ra'iisal Wasaaraha ayaa u magacaaba in ay fadhiistaan Aqalka Duqayda
Lord Chancellor (Wasiirka Caddaaladda)	Wasiirka Caddaaladdu waa Wasiiru dawli u xilsaaran magacaabidda xaakimiin cusub
Lower House (Aqalka Hoose)	Aqalka Hoose waa Baarlamaan go'aan ka gaara siyaasadda iyo shuruucda. Aqalka Hoose ee Ingiriisku waa Aqalka Komoniska
Member of Parliament (Xildhibaan)(MP)	Xildhibaanku waa wakiil dadka matalaya, oo loo doortay in uu fadhiisto Aqalka Komoniska
Metropolitan Police	Metropolitan Police waa ciidanka booliiska ee u adeega dadka London
Middle ground (Barta Dhexe)	Barta dhexe waa qodob isu keena laba fikradood oo is khilaafsan
Minister (Wasiirka)	Wasiirku waa siyaasi Dawladda meel sare kaga jira oo haya masuuliyado siyaasadda iyo waxyaabo kale la xiriira
Monarch (Boqorka ama boqoradda)	Monarch waxuu tilmaamayaa Boqoradda ama Boqorka
Mothering Sunday (Axadda Hooyooyinka)	Axadda Hooyooyinku waa maalin la xuso oo ay carruurtu hooyooyinkood mahadnaq u muujiyaan
Mugging (Boobka)	Fal dambiyeedka tuugada ah ee laga geysto dariiqa iyadoo la hanjabayo ama la xoogtamayo
National Assembly for Wales (Golaha Qaran ee Wales)	Golaha Qaran ee Wales waa halka ay wakiillada Wales ku kulmaan si ay go'aan uga gaaraan arrimaha siyaasadda la xiriira. Waxuu ku yaallaa Cardiff
National Day (Maalinta xuska Qaran)	Maalinta xuska Qaran, sida Maalinta St Patrick, waxaa lagu xusaa qarannimada waddanka iyo dhalashadiisa
New Scotland Yard	New Scotland Yard waa xarunta dhexe ee Booliiska London ee Metropolitan Police

Non-departmental Public Bodies (Hay'adaha Dawladda ee Wasaaradaha ka baxsan)	Hay'adaha dawladda ee wasaaradaha ka baxsani waa hay'ado ay dawladdu aasaastay ayna maalgeliso. Waxay aad uga xorriyad badan yihiin wasaaradaha dawladda waxaana caadi ahaan loo fasaxaa in ay hawlgalaan iyagoo ayan si toos ah u xukumin Wasiirrada iyo wasaaradaha aasaasay
Palace of Westminster (Qasriga Westminster)	Qasriga Westminster waxaa ku yaalla Aqalka Komoniska iyo Aqalka Duqayda
Parliament (Baarlamaanka)	Baarlamaanku waa halka ay ku kulmaan wakiillada qaran ee la soo doortay si ay uga wadahadlaan arrimaha jira una soo saaraan shuruucda
Parliament of Scotland (Baarlamaanka Scotland)	Baarlamaanka Scotland, oo ku yaalla Edinburgh, waxuu wakiil ka yahay dadka reer Scotland ah
Parliamentary Democracy (Dimoqraadiyadda Baarlamaaneed)	Dimoqraadiyadda baarlamaaneed waxay tilmaamaysaa waddanka ay go'aannada dawladdiisu ka soo baxaan Baarlamaan wakiillo ka kooban
Party system (Nidaamka xisbiyada)	Nidaamka xisbiyadu waa nidaam siyaasadeed oo ka kooban kooxo ay habaystaan wakiillada iyo codbixiyeyaashu. Kooxahaasi waxay caadi ahaan gaar ahaan u wadaagaan anshax iyo ujeedooyin siman
Madhabta Presbyterian Church	Madhabta Presbyterian Church waa Kaniisadda Scotland
Pressure Groups (Kooxaha Qalqaalada)	Kooxaha qalqaaladu waa kooxo dano gaar ah leh oo raba in ay siyaasiyiinta danahooda ku qalqaaliyaan
Prime Minister (Ra'iisal Wasaaraha)	Ra'iisal Wasaaruhu waa hoggaamiyaha xisbiga xukunka haya iyo guddoomiyaha Golaha wasiirrada
Proportional Representation (Matalaadda Saamiga)	Matalaadda Saamigu waa nidaamka doorashooyinka ee ay xisbiyadu kuraasta baarlamaanka ugu helaan si raacsan saamiga codadka la siiyey
Protestant	Protestant-ku waa qof diinta Kiristaanka haysta. Waxaa sidaas ah dadka haysta madhabyada Anglican Church iyo Presbyterian Church
Quango	Quango waa magac kaloo lagu tilmaamo hay'adda dawladda ee wasaaradaha ka baxsan

Queen's Speech (Khudbadda Boqoradda)	Khudbadda Boqoraddu waa mid ay Boqoraddu jeediso bilowga fadhiga cusub ee Baarlamaanka iyadoo qeexaysa siyaasadaha iyo ujeeddooyinka Dawladda
Question time (Waqtiga su'aalaha)	Waqtiga su'aaluhu waa mid si joogto ah looga qoondeeyo Aqalka Komoniska goortaasoo ay Xildhibaannadu su'aalo weydiin karaan Wasiirrada
Reformation (Dib u habaynta)	Dib u habayntu waxuu ahaa dhaqdhaqaaq jiray qarnigii lix iyo tobanaad oo Protestant-nimada ka dhigay diinta aasaasiga ah ee Ingiriiska
Remembrance Day (Maalinta Xasuusashada)	Maalinta Xasuusashada waxaa la qabtaa bisha Noofembar sanad kaste si loo xasuusto dadkii dagaalka ku dhintay
Scouse	Scouse waa lahjadda goboleed ee ay ku hadlaan dadka ku nool Liverpool
Shadow Cabinet (Golaha wasiirada ee Mucaaradka)	Golaha Wasiirrada ee Mucaaradku waa koox Xildhibaanno ah oo ka soo jeeda xisbiga mucaaradka ugu tirabadan Baarlamaanka dhexdiisa kuwaasoo u xilsaaran in ay xisbiga uga matalaan arrimaha muhiimka ah
Speaker (Afhayeenka)	Afhayeenka Aqalka Komoniska iyo Aqalka Duqayda labadoodaba waxuu guddoomiyaa doodaha baarlamaaneed
Spin (Iilinta fikradaha)	Iilinta fikraduhu waa dhan u liicinta ay afhayeennada xisbiyada siyaasadeed ku sameeyaan fikradaha ay arrimaha ka qabaan
St Andrew's Day (Maalinta St Andrew)	Maalinta xuska Qaran ee Scotland
St David's Day (Maalinta St David)	Maalinta xuska Qaran ee Wales
St George's Day (Maalinta St George)	Maalinta xuska Qaran ee England
St Patrick's Day (Maalinta St Patrick)	Maalinta xuska Qaran ee Waqooyiga Ireland iyo Jamhuuriyadda Ireland
St Valentine's Day (Maalinta St Valentine)	Maalinta St Valentine waxaa la xusaa sanad kaste bisha Febraayo waxaana lagu xusaa jacaylka iyo xiriirrada cashaaqa

Stepfamily (Qoyska dhinac xigto iskaga ah)	Qoyska dhinac xigto iskaga ahi waxuu dhashaa marka ay dad carruur lahi qof kale guursadaan
Stormont	Stormont waa magac kale oo lagu tilmaamo Baarlamaanka Waqooyiga Ireland
Supreme Governor (Guddoomiyaha Ugu sarreeya)	Guddooyimaha Ugu sarreeya waa kaalinta ay Boqorka ama Boqoraddu hayaan maadaama ay yihiin madaxa madhabta Anglican Church
Treasury (Khasnadda)	Khasnaddu waa wasaaradda dawladda ee u xilsaaran maamulka dhammaan lacagaha ay dawladdu hesho, hayso ama kharash geliso
United Nations (Qaramada Midoobay) (UN)	Qaramada Midoobay waa urur caalami ah ee u huran nabadda, ammaanka iyo xuquuqda aadamaha
United Nations Security Council (Golaha Ammaanka ee Qaramada Midoobay)	Golaha Ammaanka ee Qaramada Midoobay waa guddi ka kooban 15 xubnood oo diiradda saara ammaanka dunida. Ingiriisku waxuu ka mid yahay shantiisa xubnood ee joogtada ah
Upper House (Aqalka Sare)	Aqalka Sare waa Baarlamaan dib u eega go'aannada laga gaaro siyaasadda iyo shuruucda. Aqalka Sare ee Ingiriisku waa Aqalka Duqayda
Westminster	Westminster waa erey guud oo caadi ahaan lagu tilmaamo dawladda
Whips (Afti hubiyeyaasha)	Afti hubiyeyaashu waa Xildhibaanno hubiya in ay Xildhibaannada kale ee xisbigooda siyaasadeed u codbixiyaan si dan u ah ujeeddooyinka xisbiga
Wimbledon	Wimbledon waa tartan caan ah oo ciyaarta tenniska sanad kaste ayaana koonfurta London lagu qabtaa

ANSWERS

Answers to Revision Questions

1	In the past immigrant groups came to invade and seize land. Now people come in search of jobs and a better life
2	Aid the reconstruction effort after the Second World War
3	Irish labourers provided much of the workforce to construct the canals and railways of the UK
4	To escape religious persecution
5	Poland, Ukraine and Belarus
6	To escape the violence they faced at home
7	Ireland and the West Indies
8	West Indies
9	India and Pakistan
10	United States, Australia, South Africa, New Zealand, Hong Kong, Singapore and Malaysia
11	Uganda and South East Asia
12	1857
13	Women over the age of 30 got the right to vote in 1918
14	1928
15	There are more women than men in university
16	45%
17	Three quarters of women who have children in the UK are in paid work
18	Women receive on average 20% lower pay than men
19	Most children in Britain receive weekly pocket money
20	65%
21	35% of children do not live with both birth parents. 25% live in single parent families. 10% live with a stepfamily
22	15 million
23	Compulsory tests are carried out at ages 7, 11 and 14. GCSEs are carried out at 16. A Levels at 17 and 18
24	One in three move on to higher education
25	Two million

26	Tobacco must not be sold to anyone under the age of 16. Alcohol must not be sold to anyone under the age of 18
27	One in five
28	58.8 million
29	1.7 million
30	2.9 million
31	5.1 million
32	49.1 million
33	17%
34	2011
35	Once every ten years
36	1801
37	Because Britain was at war
38	100 years
39	7.9% of UK population
40	People of Indian descent
41	About half
42	45%
43	29%
44	75%
45	3%
46	Seven people out of ten stated their religion as Christian
47	The Anglican Church
48	1534
49	Supreme Governor
50	To maintain the Protestant religion in the United Kingdom
51	The King or Queen appoints the Archbishop of Canterbury after taking advice from the Prime Minister, which is based on a recommendation from a Church appointed committee
52	Anyone who is not Protestant
53	The Kirk
54	10%
55	Approximately 1,000 kilometres (600 miles)
56	Approximately 500 kilometres (320 miles)

57	1999
58	Baptists and Methodists
59	Highlands and Islands of Scotland
60	Wales
61	Liverpool
62	London
63	Tyneside
64	St Patrick's Day in Northern Ireland (and the Republic of Ireland)
65	St David's Day - Wales - 1 March St Patrick's Day - Northern Ireland - 17 March St George's Day - England - 23 April St Andrew's Day - Scotland - 30 November
66	Four bank holidays each year
67	Christmas Day is 25 December each year. Christmas celebrates the birth of Jesus Christ
68	On Christmas Day – 25 December
69	Often hung above doorways under which couples are expected to kiss
70	A roast turkey dinner and Christmas pudding
71	Dutch, German and Swedish settlers emigrating to America
72	Boxing Day is observed on 26 December each year. It celebrates the appreciation of work by servants and trades people
73	1 January each year
74	Coal, bread and whisky to ensure prosperity in the coming year
75	The back door is opened to release the old year, then shut and locked, and then the front door opened to let in the new year
76	New life and the coming of spring
77	Easter is celebrated in either March or April each year. It commemorates the Crucifixion and Resurrection of Jesus Christ
78	St Valentine's Day is observed on 14 February each year. On this day, couples send cards to each other. Cards are unsigned as if from secret admirers
79	Mothering Sunday is held three weeks before Easter. On this day, people remember their mothers by giving gifts and flowers and trying to make their day as enjoyable as possible
80	April Fool's Day is celebrated on 1 April each year. On this day, people play jokes on each other, but only until noon

81 Guy Fawkes Night is held on the evening of 5 November each year. The night commemorates the Gunpowder Plot of 1605 when a Catholic group plotted to bomb the Houses of Parliament and kill the King

82 Remembrance Day is observed on 11 November each year. It commemorates the memory of those who died during war

83 At the eleventh hour, of the eleventh day, of the eleventh month in 1918 (11 November 1918)

84 People wear artificial poppies in buttonholes in memory of those that lost their lives during war

85 At least once every five years

86 Member of Parliament

87 Leader of the party that forms the Government. The Prime Minister also appoints ministers of state and other important public positions

88 Primus inter pares – meaning first among equals

89 Number Ten

90 Chancellor of the Exchequer

91 Home Secretary

92 They are submitted to Parliament for approval

93 Foreign Secretary

94 10 Downing Street in London

95 About 20 MPs

96 A committee of about 20 MPs, from the party that forms the Government, that meet to decide general policies for government

97 The party with the most MPs elected into the House of Commons forms the Government

98 An unwritten constitution

99 Her Majesty's Loyal Opposition

100 To chair proceedings in the House of Commons

101 Members of Parliament may ask questions of Government Ministers

102 They are held to replace an MP when they resign or die while in office

103 Yes. Britain has a free press

104 Hansard

105 The law states that radio and television reports must be balanced and must give equal time to rival viewpoints

106 Quasi-autonomous non-governmental organisations. These are semi-independent agencies set up by the government

107 The King or Queen can only "advise, warn and encourage"

108 1952; after her father's death

109 The Queen's oldest son, the Prince of Wales

110 The Queen

111 A statement of the Government's policies for the next session in parliament. The statement is entirely provided by the Prime Minister

112 Opening and closing of parliament and reading the "Queen's (or King's) Speech"

113 Holders of high office within the Government, the armed forces and the Church of England

114 In the Palace of Westminster

115 The House of Commons is sometimes called the Lower House; and the House of Lords, the Upper House

116 645

117 Represent their constituency; help create and shape new laws; scrutinise and comment on government activities; debate important national issues

118 Tickets to the public galleries can be obtained from your local MP or by queuing on the day at the public entrance

119 The Speaker is elected to the position by fellow MPs

120 A small group of MPs that ensure discipline and attendance of MPs at voting time in the House of Commons

121 By being either peers of the realm (hereditary aristocrats), or as reward for special public service

122 1957

123 A member of the House of Lords who has been appointed by the Prime Minister – but only for the member's lifetime

124 To examine in detail, and at greater leisure, new laws proposed by the House of Commons, and to suggest amendments or changes

125 The "first past the post" system

126 The candidate must win the most votes out of all candidates

127 Proportional representation is used in the Scottish Parliament, Welsh Assembly and Northern Ireland Assembly

128 Pressure groups are voluntary groups of ordinary citizens. Lobby groups generally represent commercial, industrial and professional organisations

129	No, but they may declare it incompatible with human rights
130	They are appointed by the Lord Chancellor, from nominations put forward by existing judges
131	The Metropolitan Police
132	New Scotland Yard in London
133	Elected local councillors and magistrates, and by the Home Secretary
134	The police are organised locally, usually each county has its own police force
135	Any independent manager or administrator who has a job requiring them to carry out Government policy
136	Neutrality and professionalism
137	In the early 19th century
138	To provide community services in their local area, such as education, planning, health, environmental, transport, fire services, refuse collection, libraries and housing
139	From central government taxation; only 20% of funding is provided through council tax
140	May each year
141	The programme began in 1997. The Welsh Assembly and the Scottish Parliament were established in 1999
142	Policies governing defence, foreign affairs, taxation and social security. This doesn't exclude these topics from being debated in other assemblies
143	In Cardiff
144	60 Assembly Members
145	1979
146	1997
147	129 Members of the Scottish Parliament
148	Unlike the Welsh Assembly, the Scottish Parliament is able to pass legislation on anything not specifically reserved for Westminster
149	Stormont; after the building where the assembly meets
150	1922
151	1998
152	108 members
153	1949
154	To protect human rights and seek solutions to problems facing European society

155 To put all their coal and steel production under the control of a single authority. This was done in the belief that it would reduce the likelihood of another war

156 1973 – This was after being vetoed twice by France

157 For member states to become a single market

158 Citizens of any EU member state have the right to travel to any EU country as long as they have a valid passport or identity card

159 Citizens of any EU member state have the right to work in any EU country, and must be offered employment under the same conditions as citizens of that state

160 An influential body in the EU made up of government ministers from each member state. It has powers to propose new laws and take decisions about how the EU is run

161 Brussels

162 To scrutinise and debate the proposals, decisions and expenditure of the European Commission

163 A general requirement that must be introduced in EU member states within a specific time frame

164 A specific rule that automatically has force in all EU member states, and that overrides national legislation

165 1.7 billion people

166 54 member states

167 An international organisation that works to prevent war and maintain peace and security

168 It is a member of the UN Security Council

169 Full civic rights to vote in all elections and duties such as jury service

170 A candidate must be a citizen of the United Kingdom, Irish Republic or Commonwealth and be 21 years or over

171 By completing an electoral registration form. These forms are sent to households in September and October each year

172 Contact details can be found in the phone book or local library. Alternatively, representatives hold local 'surgery' sessions, often on Saturday mornings

MARKING SHEET

	Test 1	Test 2	Test 3	Test 4	Test 5	Test 6	Test 7	Test 8	Test 9	Test 10
1										
2										
3										
4										
5										
6										
7										
8										
9										
10										
11										
12										
13										
14										
15										
16										
17										
18										
19										
20										
21										
22										
23										
24										
Total										

SCORING GUIDE

Check your test results using this scoring guide.

Less than 6	**Very poor** – Do not take any further practice tests until significant revision has been completed.
7–12	**Unsatisfactory** – Considerable gaps in knowledge. Further revision of study materials required.
13–17	**Good** – Not quite ready yet. Revise your weak areas to complete your knowledge.
18 or more	**Excellent** – Well done! You are above the pass mark and are now ready to sit the official test.

PRACTICE TEST ANSWERS

	Test 1	Test 2	Test 3	Test 4	Test 5	Test 6	Test 7	Test 8	Test 9	Test 10
1	C	C	C	A	B	B & D	A	B	A & B	A
2	B	D	C	D	C	C	C	B	C	B
3	C	A	D	A	B	D	C	B	C	B
4	B	B	B	C	B	A	A	C	C	B
5	C	C	B	B	C	C	B	A	C	D
6	C	B	B	B	C	B	B	A	B	C
7	D	A	B	C	A & C	B	C	A	A	D
8	D	C	A	B	D	A	B	B	D	D
9	C	B	D	A	B	D	C	D	C	B
10	C	B	D	D	B	C	C	D	C	B
11	B	D	B	A	D	C	D	B	D	B
12	D	B	C	C	A	B	A	B	A	A
13	D	C	A	A	B	A	B	A & C	A & B	B
14	C	C	D	B	A	B	B & C	A	B	A
15	A	B	B	C	D	B	A & B	A	B	B & C
16	D	B	D	A	B	A	B	C	A	D
17	A & D	D	B	C & D	B	C	B	C	A	B
18	B & D	B	B	A	D	C	A	B	C	D
19	C	A	B & D	A	A	D	D	D	C	D
20	B	C & D	C	A	D	B	C	D	A	D
21	C	B	D	B	B	D	A	D	B	C
22	B	B	A	C	A	C	D	D	C	D
23	A	D	D	B	B & D	C	A	A	C	A
24	B	C	B	A	A	A	D	C	B	A
Total										

British Citizenship Test
Study Centre

- Get the latest information about the Life in the UK test
- Take a free test to check your knowledge
- Check out hints and tips
- Read reviews and tips from other readers